Twenty Challenges to Enlightenment

Twenty Challenges to Enlightenment

Lectures by
Dharma Master Cheng Yen

Translated by Lin Sen-shou
English edited by Douglas Shaw and Hu Tsung-hsiang

Translated by Lin Sen-shou
English edited by Douglas Shaw and Hu Tsung-hsiang
Inside art by Mi Xiong Kuan Hung Buddhist Arts Center
Cover design by Chang Shih-ming

Published by the Tzu Chi Cultural Publishing Co.
Foreign Language Publications Department
Address: 19, Alley7, Lane217, Sec.3, Zhongxiao East Rd., Taipei, Taiwan
Telephone: 886-2-2898-9888

Printed March 2001
Sixth Printing June 2008
ISBN:957-8300-74-3

靜思文化
JING JI PUBLICATIONJ   http:// www.jingsi.com.tw

TABLE OF CONTENTS

It is difficult…

IT IS DIFFICULT
FOR THE POOR TO GIVE GENEROUSLY

The tranquillity of the early morning is broken by the sound of people chanting the Buddhist sutras. The sound comes from within the main sanctuary of the Abode of Still Thoughts [the headquarters of the Tzu Chi Foundation in Hualien, eastern Taiwan]. There, practitioners engage in morning prayers, meditation and self-reflection. Outside the Abode are pilgrims who have come to pay tribute. Whether outside or inside the Abode, any place is a good place for carrying out spiritual cultivation. Spiritual cultivation means that no matter where you are, you strive to make your mind tranquil and your behavior proper, thus reaching a serene state of mind. The external environment should not affect your self-cultivation.

We encounter many difficulties when we deal with worldly affairs, and even more difficulties when we are learning the ways of the Buddha. Some difficulties lie in carrying out the Buddhist teachings one has learned, some lie in saying the proper things, and some difficulties, perhaps the biggest, pertain to keeping one's mind sincere and respectful. These difficulties are included in what the Buddha pointed out as the "Twenty Difficulties on the Way to Attaining Buddhahood" in Chapter

Twelve of the *Forty-Two Chapter Sutra*. Of the Twenty Difficulties that the Buddha enumerated, the first one is, "It is difficult for the poor to give generously."

THERE ARE MANY THORNS ON THE PATH OF GIVING

Giving generously is a means of spiritual cultivation in Buddhism and also the first principle in the Six Paramitas, or Six Ways to Reach Nirvana. It is an expression of love. It means the elimination of one's ego and the expansion of one's heart to care for all people.

Giving generously sounds easy enough, but to some people it is rather difficult. Anywhere in the world, there is always a need for people to give generously. A country or society where people do not help or give to one another is no place for human beings.

When we learn Buddhism, we must seek pure love and perfect the art of giving, and this is the essence of giving generously. The Buddha said that it was difficult for the poor to give generously, and this is still true today. Poor people often lack even the necessities of daily life, so how can they have enough left over to give to others? They may have loving, generous hearts, but because they lack material goods, their good intentions often cannot be actualized. Thus, it is difficult for the poor to give generously. However, is it truly so difficult to give when you are poor? A true story shows otherwise.

There was once a young patient in Tzu Chi Hospital. He had been in a serious car accident, and a spinal cord injury left him completely paralyzed. Doctors predicted that he would never recover full use of his limbs. Nevertheless, the doctors still treated him with care, and nurses and volunteers helped him attentively and encouraged him. I myself went to see him frequently to give him moral support. Also, he was lucky to have a kind sister-in-law, who cared for him like a mother. With so many people concerned about his well-being, the young man finally accepted the fact of his disability. Not only that, he regained his confidence and resolved not to be imprisoned by his crippled body.

When he had taken on such a positive attitude, a miracle occurred: he was able to move his arms. "If I can make it into a wheelchair," he vowed, "I will help other people by becoming a volunteer!"

With much hard work, he was finally able to sit up in a wheelchair. He wanted to organize a self-help club for people, especially young people, with spinal injuries, because he knew that they suffered a great deal of mental agony. He hoped that with the establishment of this organization, disabled people could encourage each other and help each other face the world bravely. Every disabled person, he believed, had the potential to lead a life that was as happy and fulfilling as that of a healthy person. With help from Tzu Chi social workers, the club was finally established. The young man designed and edited a monthly newsletter for all club members.

Although he did not have full use of his hands and could not write, he never gave up on his goals. He asked for help from rehabilitation specialists, who patiently taught him to use finger caps to type on a computer. He typed slowly and with extreme difficulty, but finally completed a newsletter. I was deeply touched when I first saw that newsletter, especially when I thought of all the obstacles he had to overcome. Many healthy people do not even bother to learn computer skills, while he had the patience and perseverance to go through with it.

Today, because of his enthusiasm, many people with spinal injuries have become members of the club and benefited from the support of people like themselves. With a strong will and constant effort, he was able to help others despite his own limitations. This proves that giving generously is not necessarily impossible for people with fewer resources. However, lack of material means can still be a hindrance to giving.

The young man noticed that some members, completely paralyzed and confined to bed, were unable to turn themselves over and had no family members to help them do so. He was worried that they would develop bedsores, and so he resolved to buy automatic beds that could turn patients onto their sides or backs. One year, he tried to raise money by selling Chinese New Year ornaments. He made a little over ten thousand dollars, but that was a minuscule amount compared to the hundreds of thousands of dollars that an automatic bed cost. Undiscouraged, he went from store to store in the hope of raising the money from shopkeepers, but he was received coldly. My friends, this young man had the best intentions, but he was unable to realize them. This illustrates what the Buddha meant when he said, "It is difficult for the poor to give generously."

We who are healthy have the strength and independence to do good deeds. In everyday life, if we would all consume a little less food and goods, then what was saved would be enough to help a lot of needy people. But for someone with a spinal injury or any kind of handicap, it is not that easy to use even less than the little that they have. So we should cherish the wonderful opportunity we have to help others. Think how lucky we are to be unhindered from doing good deeds. Those of us who are blessed with good health should give generously now. We mustn't wait until it is too late, when we have exhausted our blessings and are no longer able to give.

Spiritual cultivation involves breaking through diverse difficulties, and the path to enlightenment is not always smooth. When we encounter obstacles, we must overcome them with perseverance and faith. Even the Buddha underwent more than a decade of hardship and mental struggle to complete his spiritual cultivation. Before attaining enlightenment, he first had to resist and subdue the evil forces. "Evil" is any kind of spiritual obstacle. When we are learning Buddhism, it is natural that we will confront all sorts of obstacles, either from outside or within our own minds.

If You Blindly Drift Through Life, You Create Your Own Obstacles

It is easy to drift along with the current of life and death, but it is quite difficult to go against it. Most ordinary people are completely lost in the cycle of reincarnation. They do not know why they came into this world, and they never want to talk about where life comes from. Since they will not explore all this, they pass their days in confusion and ignorance. There are wealthy people who indulge themselves in extravagant lifestyles, but refuse to give even a small part of their fortune to help others and to do something meaningful.

I once heard a Tzu Chi commissioner [the members of the foundation who actively collect donations and seek out those who need help] talk about a friend of hers whose wealth was beyond calculation. The commissioner asked her friend whether he knew what kind of work the foundation was doing.

"Sure, I've heard," he replied.

"Then would you like to become a Tzu Chi member and do some good work?" asked the commissioner.

"But I've done so many good things already," her friend announced. "Buddhism teaches people to form good relationships with each other, and that's exactly what I've done. Just think, I host banquets all the time, and each banquet costs tens of thousands of dollars! Am I not generous? I even give thousand-dollar tips to the waitresses! But people still criticize me for being stingy! In what way am I not generous?"

He was extremely generous, but he did not know that the money he spent on extravagant dinners could have helped so many people struggling to survive in destitution and sickness, sick old people shivering in broken-down houses, widows and orphans. Also unknown to him was that one dinner less would have meant one more life saved in the hospital. Perhaps none of this ever crossed his mind. Unenlightened, he simply drifted through his luxurious life without ever really opening his eyes to the world. There are so many people like him.

As they are carried along by the current of the cycle of reincarnation, so many unfortunate people lose their innate conscience. All good things are far from them, and it is extremely difficult to get them to do things that benefit other people. This is a personal obstacle to spiritual cultivation, and we have to pity these poor people for their profound lack of spirituality and wisdom.

WITH GREAT PERSEVERANCE, YOU CAN GO AGAINST THE CURRENT OF LIFE AND DEATH

In life or in spiritual cultivation, as long as we persevere, we can overcome any external obstacles, even in the most adverse situations. As in swimming, those who know how to swim can go against the current, whereas those who do not are in danger of drowning.

Learning to behave like the Buddha means breaking through difficulties and understanding where we come from and where we are going. However, before we can answer the question of life and death, the most important thing is to guard over our present thoughts. If we dwell only on the past and the future, we will easily be trapped in our own distractions and fantasies. Instead, we should establish a clear direction and a firm footing for the present moment, because "If the first step of a long journey is even slightly wrong, you may miss your goal by miles."

The authentic Buddhist dharma is the most genuine Truth for this world and the world beyond. In the cycle of reincarnation, we rarely come into this world in human form. Thus, we must remember how fortunate we are to be here in this lifetime and to be able to learn the Buddha's teachings. Therefore, we should not merely seek release from the cycle of reincarnation, but more importantly, we must earnestly practice the dharma we have learned. Learning to behave like the Buddha means carrying out what we have learned of his teachings. Do not fear external obstacles or hardships—they can train our endurance. A person with perseverance and courage will not succumb to obstacles. He will retain his determination and maintain his course, regardless of external hindrances.

A commissioner once told me a story. "Today, I was entrusted by someone to donate NT$15,000 [US$450] to Tzu Chi Hospital to help them purchase a hospital bed," she recounted. "What really moved me was that the money came from a truly remarkable person."

So I asked her, "What kind of person was this?"

"A handicapped man who is receiving our long-term aid for people with low income."

"If he is receiving financial aid from us, how did he come to have so much money?" I asked.

"I asked him the same question when he gave me the money," she replied. "He told me that every month, out of the NT$3,000 we gave him, he would save at least NT$300. After some time, he had around NT$8,000 saved up. Along with some money that his relatives and neighbors gave him at Chinese New Year, he had altogether approximately NT$14,000. When he received his aid for this month, he took out some of the money to add to what he had saved up and finally reached the sum of NT$15,000. He did this because he had often heard about other people donating money to buy hospital beds, and he really wanted to do the same. It was his constant wish to become one of the people who pitched in to help support the hospital. Therefore, he was overjoyed today to finally be able to hand me the money."

What a touching story! Just think, he was disabled and living on financial aid, yet he still saved one-tenth of his monthly pension for a good cause. Imagine, it must have taken years to close the gap between $300 and $15,000. However, once he had decided to perform this good deed, he was not discouraged by the time it would take to achieve it. Just think! Although it was not easy for a person in his situation to give generously, he was able to overcome his limitations.

If You Have the Will, You Can Overcome Your Desires

It is very difficult to go against the flow of the cycle of reincarnation and all the worldly desires that it brings. A swimmer must have courage and perseverance to swim against the current and reach the other shore. The same can be said about spiritual cultivation. We must not go along with the flow of reincarnation or be driven by our greed for worldly pleasures. Of all the difficulties that we must overcome, the most important is to eliminate our desires.

We desire all sorts of things: money, sensual pleasures, prestige, food, sleep, etc. If we try to satisfy these desires, we become common people who just drift blindly through life. Eliminating these desires requires a lot of effort. Although it sounds very difficult, it is not hard for people who have faith and courage. I ask all of you to persevere and try your best to go against the stream of life and death, to break through all obstacles, both those in your mind and in the outside world. As long as you are not lost in the current of life and death, you will be able to give generously even if you are poor.

Particularly in Tzu Chi, there are many poor people who are committed to doing good deeds and are as willing to give as the wealthier people are. "Giving generously" includes not only donating material goods, but also doing good deeds through volunteer service.

The Buddha was referring to most common people when he said, "It is difficult for the poor to give generously." But people who learn Buddhism have seen through everything in this world, so they are not consumed by the need to fulfill their desires and can thus spend their lives doing good deeds. Take, for example, the disabled person who was able to save enough money to donate a hospital bed. Although he was poor, it was not difficult for him because of his determination to offer generously.

The Buddha said, "The mind alone creates everything." The buddhas of the past, present and future attained buddhahood through their minds. If we make up our mind to do something, what seems difficult will not be difficult anymore.

There is a saying, "Nothing is difficult if you work hard." During the Buddha's time, a poor old woman bartered her long hair for an oil lamp, so that she could keep a light burning as an offering to the Buddha. That was her way of giving. Another woman was so poor that all she had was the ragged dress she wore, so she cut off a piece of cloth from the collar as an offering to the Buddha. In the Tzu Chi world, there are many stories that show that as long as you have the will, you can achieve anything.

For people who have many desires, giving generously is an extremely difficult thing, but for people with determination, no obstacle is insurmountable.

IT IS DIFFICULT
FOR THE RICH TO LEARN
THE WAY TO ENLIGHTENMENT

The purpose of spiritual cultivation is to achieve a state of serenity. However, it is often difficult to find a quiet moment at the Abode of Still Thoughts. It is most peaceful in the morning, but even then trains, airplanes and trucks can be heard roaring by in the distance, disrupting the quietude. People who have calmed down become very sensitive and every noise in the surrounding environment is distinctly audible. During meditation, if someone sitting next to them breathes a little heavier, they can hear it. Many disturbances prevent us from arriving at a perfect state of serenity, and this is one of the difficulties that people face in learning Buddhism.

GREED, ANGER AND DELUSION BLOCK THE PATH TO ENLIGHTENMENT

The second difficulty to attaining buddhahood is, "It is difficult for the rich to learn the path of enlightenment." It means that rich, prestigious people have a difficult time learning the way of enlightenment. While ordinary people may have faults such as greed, anger, delusion, arrogance and suspicion, rich people are even more prone to be arrogant, thus failing to reach the Confucian ideal of "Be wealthy and courteous at the same time." This is why the Buddha observed that it was difficult for the rich to learn the way of enlightenment. Even if wealthy people really want to learn, they are likely to encounter more obstacles. For example, many wealthy people are very busy and do not have the time to contemplate what true religion is. Even if they do have some kind of faith, they only pray that business will be more profitable or that everything will go their way. This is an example of mistaken faith.

Some businesspeople believe that they have to worship certain folk gods. They are often extremely generous when it comes to donating money for the construction of new temples to these local deities.

Once a famous person paid me a visit. He brought along incense sticks, paper money [burnt as an offering to the gods] and a gold medallion [to hang on a god's statue]. He asked me, "Where is your incense burner?"

I replied, "We don't burn paper money here."

Surprised, he said, "Aren't we always supposed to burn paper money in temples?"

"No, not in Buddhist temples," I answered.

Later on, he presented a red envelope with the gold medallion inside. He asked me on which statue of the Buddha or the bodhisattvas he should hang it.

I explained, "We don't practice this in Buddhism. The Buddha and the bodhisattvas don't like to wear this kind of thing, so there is no need for it."

"This is very strange," he opined. "When I go to other temples, I always give gold medallions to hang on the statues of the gods."

I said to him, "Then I'll keep the medallion and use it for charity work. Will that be alright?"

He then said to me, "Yes, do whatever you want with it."

After he had prostrated himself before the Buddha's statue, I invited him to sit in the reception room. He was here on business and was supposed to listen to my report on our foundation's charity work. Instead, he kept on talking about how much money he had donated to temples or how his grandparents finally found a good burial site after consulting a geomancer.

Listening to him, I sighed inwardly. "The Buddha was right: it is indeed difficult for the rich to learn the path of enlightenment."

The Buddha once said, "If the rich do not have wisdom, their fortune will diminish." Consider the cases of people who became rich overnight. How long can their wealth last? We often see the *nouveaux riches* flaunting their wealth. They buy the most expensive clothes, but they lack the good sense to dress simply and elegantly. They decorate themselves with costly jewelry, only to appear vulgar and overdressed. They travel around the world, only to brag about the many places they have been to afterwards. I honestly feel sorry for such people.

The rich should have the wisdom to understand that they should contribute to society what they earned from it. If they can do so, they will certainly be respected and become valuable people, people who are able to realize their potential to do good and help others.

If You Are Sincere Enough, You Can Do Anything

The Buddha said, "If a rich man has no wisdom, he will soon lose his wealth." For Buddhists, money and ability must be combined with the wisdom to know what to do with them. But how many people in this world have that wisdom? That was why the Buddha said, "It is difficult for the rich to learn the way of enlightenment."

However, in Tzu Chi this is no longer a difficulty. There are many wealthy and distinguished people who enthusiastically support the Tzu Chi missions. Once, four government officials—Premier Lee, Interior Minister Hsu, former Taiwan Provincial Governor Chiu, and Education Minister Mao—came together to the Abode of Still Thoughts in Hualien. After visiting our various establishments and seeing and hearing all about the work Tzu Chi is doing, they were deeply impressed and immediately decided to become Tzu Chi members.

The next day, during a government celebration for Chinese New Year, Governor Chiu called on all levels of government employees to emulate the Tzu Chi spirit. He said, "If everyone has the Tzu Chi spirit, Taiwan will become a better place to live in." Premier Lee and Minister Hsu also mentioned that they had become members of the Tzu Chi Foundation.

All these prominent government officials were delighted to become part of Tzu Chi. In fact, many Tzu Chi Honorary Board members are people of high status who see the Tzu Chi spirit as their moral guidance.

The Buddha said it was difficult for the rich to learn the way of enlightenment—but that is not so for those who have joined Tzu Chi. Here their innate goodness is put to use, they learn the wisdom to give generously to society, and they are able to eliminate their arrogance.

People from all around Taiwan constantly visit the Abode of Still Thoughts. Groups of people set out early in the morning on pilgrimages to the Abode. Rich or poor, they chant the Buddha's name together and prostrate themselves at every third step. They walk together on the Tzu Chi Path of the Bodhisattvas. In these groups, rich people who are willing to offer generously and humble themselves learn that the way of enlightenment is no longer difficult.

Your fate is not immutable. Although there are many obstacles, with perseverance you can break through and transform your fate and karma. That's why the Buddha said, "Mind alone creates everything." There is nothing that cannot be altered for the sincere learner of the way to enlightenment. We should cultivate both our blessings and our wisdom. Giving generously is important, but so is learning the way to enlightenment. A life with abundant blessings and wisdom is the most valuable.

IT IS DIFFICULT
TO FACE DEATH

I f you ask people what they are busy with day in and day out, they would most probably answer, "Making a living"—that is, keeping themselves alive. All people value their own existence. It is hard for people to give up even their possessions, let alone their own lives. Thus, the Buddha told us that it is difficult to face death.

ORDINARY PEOPLE CANNOT BEAR SEPARATION OR DEATH

Everyone understands that birth, aging, illness and death are in the natural course of life. Yet when life nears its end, it is still so hard to let go.

In a hospital, a doctor may be in a dilemma after reaching a diagnosis, unable to decide if he should tell a terminal cancer patient the truth about his illness. Even breaking the news to the patient's family can be a struggle, since family members are normally devastated. It is harrowing for them to conceal their pain and try to console the patient, well knowing that their loved one is on the brink of death.

Even when I see patients who are seriously ill or dying, I cannot bring myself to say, "Let go of every-thing and leave in peace." Who would have the courage to say something like that? It is not easy to tell people to let go of life.

RELIGIOUS PEOPLE GIVE THEIR LIVES TO PROTECT THEIR FAITH AND THUS ACHIEVE ENLIGHTENMENT

It is hard to risk doing something when you know that you may sacrifice your life. However, for the truly religious person, this is not in the least difficult. In the past, countless people have given their lives to defend their faith.

Purnamaitrayiputra went to the Buddha one day and piously prostrated himself. The disciple asked the Buddha to allow him to go the most barbaric area in the deep south to propagate his teachings.

"Promoting my teachings is a trying mission, and you must be able to endure the unendurable," the Buddha said to him. "Do you have the perseverance to be patient and remain faithful to my teachings?"

"Since I have become a Buddhist monk, it is my calling to devote my life to all living beings," Purnamaitrayiputra replied. "If I am willing to give my life, there is nothing that I cannot endure."

"It is commendable to have this kind of spirit," the Buddha said. "Nevertheless, those southern barbarians cannot be reasoned with. What if they do not accept what you preach?"

"I can try to persuade them gradually and persistently," the faithful disciple replied.

"What if they not only do not accept you, but resist you?"

"If they resist me, I will have to endure it."

The Buddha tested him again, "What if they taunt and ridicule you?"

"I will thank them for abusing me only verbally and not physically."

"What if they beat you?"

"Then I must thank them even more for not injuring me with knives or clubs."

"What if they do injure you with knives or clubs?"

"I still have to thank them for only injuring my skin and flesh and not taking my life."

"What if they kill you?"

"I still have to feel grateful to them. We undergo all kinds of suffering because of our bodies. I have heard the Buddha's lectures and understand the Truth. I am ready to give away my body and my life for all living beings and for the dharma. If I die, then my life has come to a dignified end. Therefore, I have to thank them for helping me complete my journey on the Path of the Bodhisattvas."

This is what I call a truly religious man! He was fully aware that his path would be rough, but he still chose to walk on it anyway. Insults and beatings he received with gratitude. To propagate the Buddha's teachings and promote the well-being of all people, he had neither fear nor regrets, even if it meant losing his life. In fact, he would even thank them for helping him to achieve his spiritual goals.

For practitioners on the Path of the Bodhisattvas, giving up their lives is not at all difficult. This is because they have a transcendent view of life and fear no suffering.

TRANSCEND LIFE AND DEATH AND USE YOUR POTENTIAL

In their insatiable pursuit of wealth and fame, many ordinary people often act as if they were courageous. If they see some problem in society, they lead protests and demonstrations to stir up people's attention. But in the face of real danger, they are the first to run. Only truly religious people who have looked beyond life and death are able and willing to risk great danger and sacrifice their own lives for the well-being and enlightenment of all people.

Who does not die? No life is permanent. Knowing that all lives eventually come to an end, why not make the best use of our lives while we still can?

A religious believer must have a mind that transcends life and death. Although the Buddha told us that it is difficult to face death, we should still be able to make the best use of our potential to do good and give meaning to our lives, even if that means sacrificing our lives for others. In this way, we will have overcome a seemingly unconquerable obstacle, a rare and commendable feat.

IT IS DIFFICULT
TO READ THE BUDDHIST SUTRAS

There seem to be so many difficult things in life. Sometimes it is hard just to open a bottle or walk on a wet floor. In the end, every little thing we do seems to be difficult in some way. But in fact, the real difficulties in life are those which I have been and will be talking about.

Actually, if we are determined enough, we can accomplish even the really difficult tasks. On the other hand, if we do not put our hearts into the job, we will give up for the slightest reasons. Take walking across a wet floor for instance: we are afraid to walk on it for fear of slipping, which can easily be avoided if we are careful and walk cautiously. How difficult can that be? If we are always held back by the prospect of difficulty, we will achieve nothing in life.

LANGUAGE IS A DIFFICULTY

Now let's talk about the fourth difficulty to attaining Buddhahood: "It is difficult to read the Buddhist sutras." Does this mean that the sutras are hard to come by? Some people would say: "What is so difficult about that? Generous benefactors sponsor the printing and distribution of sutras, so many that it is hard to find a place to store them." Indeed, with such easy access to the sutras, why did the Buddha say it is hard to read them?

For us contemporary readers, the difficulty in fact lies in the abstruse nature of the sutras. It is not easy for modern people to read the sutras in depth and comprehend them thoroughly. Modern Chinese people are only familiar with vernacular Chinese and are not versed in the classical language. There is a big language gap that prevents people from fully understanding the contents of classical texts.

The reason that the Buddha said it was difficult to read the Buddhist sutras was because there *were* no printed sutras in his time. The Buddha based his teachings on the social background, the people to whom he spoke and the situation they were in. No matter who he met, he was always able to teach and guide them with his wisdom. Such was the nature of the Buddha's teachings — insights derived from wise observations, occasioned by different people and different situations — that they were never written down in advance. It was after the Buddha had passed away that his disciples compiled the teachings that had been passed down orally.

At that time, Mahakasyapa and Ananda, two of the Buddha's disciples, undertook the compilation of the Buddha's teachings. Ananda recited them from memory, and other disciples with good memories repeated what they had heard from Ananda to other people in short, simple sentences. As described in the *Wonderful Lotus Sutra*, if a person hears a sutra and repeats it for others to hear, that person will accumulate merits. If each listener then tells the sutra to others and they in turn continue to pass it on, then even the fiftieth person who hears and retells the teachings will accumulate merits. The meaning of this is that we must listen to the sutras attentively and remember them well, so that we may pass the dharma on to others.

TIME AND DISTANCE ARE DIFFICULTIES

The Tzu Chi Foundation started from "nothing" and gradually became "something." Since Tzu Chi was the first organization of its kind in Taiwan, there was no precedent for it to follow. The foundation was painstakingly and enthusiastically built in pursuit of its ideals. Many people came to visit. They then shared with others what they saw of and felt about Tzu Chi, so that others could also learn about the foundation and be inspired to join in the missions of Tzu Chi.The compilation of the sutras was also a process that started from "nothing" and ended up with "something." After the Buddha passed away, his teachings were preserved orally, and it was not until much later that the sutras were inscribed on palm leaves in Sanskrit. Even then, they were only simple records of the sutras. We can then understand the reasons why the Buddha said, "It is difficult to read the Buddhist sutras." First, in the one hundred years after his death, there were no sutras to read. Second, can these sutras, passed down orally, be accurate records of what the Buddha actually said? It is hard to say. For example, I speak to you in the Taiwanese dialect and someone transcribes it in Chinese characters. The result is unlikely to be a verbatim transcript, because I am speaking in a dialect for which many words or expressions cannot be found in written Chinese [all Chinese writing is based on the Mandarin dialect, which is quite different from Taiwanese]. In addition, sutras date back thousands of years before our time, so it is even more difficult to grasp the true meaning of the Buddha's teachings in the sense of how language was employed in his time and what meanings the words contained.

There are abundant supplies of sutras in Taiwan, but not necessarily so in other places. Tzu Chi members of our United States branches are always delighted to receive their monthly copies of the *Tzu Chi Monthly*, *Tzu Chi Companion* or other publications. These publications are hard to come by since the number of copies sent from Taiwan each month is limited. Therefore, Tzu Chi members in the United States regard them as rare and precious. Geographical distance, then, as opposed to distance through time, is also a difficulty that prevents people from reading the Buddhist sutras.

UNWILLINGNESS AND INACTION CREATE MORE DIFFICULTIES

I imagine that if someone does not have the desire, then even if the most wondrous sutra were sitting within a hand's reach and could be read in one sitting, he would not lift a hand to do it. Is this not a difficulty in reading the Buddhist sutras? In other words, the difficulty that the Buddha referred to lies within our hearts.

If we do not have in our hearts the will to learn, we will not act on it. Nothing can be gained without labor, let alone the wisdom contained in the sutras that will help us transcend this lowly world.

In Taiwan, complete collections of the sutras, including the twelve sutras and the *Tripitaka*, can easily be found. Furthermore, many scholars have translated the sutras from classical Chinese into modern Chinese. However, if we lack the desire, it will always be difficult to read and comprehend the sutras, even if we are surrounded by them.

A sutra is a way, and a way is a road. Not only must we study the sutras, but we also have to travel the roads—that is, practice the ways conveyed in the sutras. If we fail to do so, the distance between humans and the Buddha will remain immeasurably large. One who learns Buddhism must understand it thoroughly and practice it earnestly. It is my wish that you all march fearlessly along the path pointed out by the sutras. If we are deterred by the mere mention of a floor being wet and hard to walk on, how can we travel the limitless path of Buddhism? With the right mindset and constant practice of the teachings contained in the sutras, we will be able to reach the end of volumes and volumes of sutras—the enlightened state of all buddhas.

Practice What You Learn

These days, people generally enjoy a higher level of education than our predecessors, but not many people really study hard. Even rarer are those who are able to both study hard and apply the theories they learn to practical use. Some students major in agriculture at school but end up in business; others study business but work in the industrial sector after graduation. In short, very few people can devote themselves to their discipline and make use of what they learn. Imagine, then, how much more difficult it is to study the dharma, the Buddhist teachings, which requires a mind that transcends the world.

If we cannot pay attention to and perfect our behavior and studies as a person, how can we be good Buddhists? Although sutras can be easily obtained these days thanks to advanced printing technology, there are still few people who can comprehend the dogmas and apply them to their daily lives. This is why the Buddha said it was difficult to read his teachings.

Let us go back to the time of the Buddha. The Buddha had a disciple named Sronakotivimsa. He was the only son of a rich man, and his parents doted on him. When he was born, his parents hired so many servants to look after him that his feet never touched the ground. How does a person live from infancy to adulthood without ever having set foot on the ground? Naturally, there was always somebody waiting on him, and at home he was carried about in a sedan chair. Fine hair grew from his soles due to lack of use. We can see what a comfortable life he led and how his parents pampered him.

Once the Buddha was lecturing in the Abode of Jetavana [a lecture hall and residence constructed for the Buddha and his monks]. Although Sronakotivimsa hardly ever went out, he had heard that the Buddha was an enlightened man and longed to meet him. He told his parents that he wished to go visit the Buddha. His parents felt that this was a rare opportunity for him to broaden his intellectual scope, so they had the servants carry him in his sedan chair to the abode.

Of course the young man's traveling style did not go unnoticed by the Buddha, so he talked to him about the impermanence of life and how we should make meaningful use of our lives. After hearing what the Buddha said, Sronakotivimsa realized acutely that ever since he was born he had never been of any use to anyone. He was frightened, because life was so impermanent and he might easily lose the chance to make something of his life. He felt that he was unqualified to live in society anymore, so he asked if the Buddha would allow him to become a monk.

"If you become a monk, you must live together with the sangha [the assembly of monks and nuns]," the Buddha reminded Sronakotivimsa. "Your behavior, speech and thought must conform with those of the other monks, so that you can live harmoniously with them."

The young man earnestly wanted to become a monk and expressed his willingness to live with the sangha. To prove his determination, he stood up and took the first step in his life, with his feet touching the ground. He walked over to the Buddha and prostrated himself. He confessed that he had accomplished nothing in his life, and he said that he was now willing to realize his potentials. He wanted to do what others could not do and endure what no one else could endure.

LIKE A MUSICAL STRING

Sronakotivimsa was diligent and conscientious. He cleaned the monks' residence and kept things in order. Whenever he had time, he would recite the Buddha's teachings and could always be heard chanting the dharma. He slept less and less, finding it a waste of time even to close his eyes. Not one single second was to go by unused.

Someone told the Buddha how Sronakotivimsa was studying so hard that he would not go out to beg for alms or go to sleep at night, and that he could be risking his life if he went on like that. The Buddha then went to Sronakotivimsa's cell. "You are working very hard at cultivating yourself! Tell me, what was your favorite hobby at home?"

Sronakotivimsa replied, "I liked to play the lute."

"What happens if the strings are too loose?" the Buddha asked.

"They won't make any sound."

"And if the strings are to tight?"

"That's not good because the strings will easily snap."

"Under what condition will the lute play most beautifully?"

"When the strings are not too loose and not too tight, then the lute will sound the best."

"The same goes for spiritual cultivation: you should be neither slack nor overly diligent. Too much or too little are both dangerous. The best way is moderation. Therefore, you must readjust your life and follow a more regular routine. Concentrate when you are cultivating yourself and don't be indolent, but rest when you must. If you can keep regular hours, understand the dharma with your heart, and put what you have learned into practice in everyday life, then your spiritual cultivation will be complete."

Modern people should learn Buddhism in the same way that Sronakotivimsa learned from the Buddha. If one only reads the sutras but does not carry out their teachings, then one fails to combine theory with life. Therefore, "It is difficult to read the Buddhist sutras" really means that it is difficult to fully understand and practice the Buddhist teachings.

Nowadays, people generally enjoy a higher standard of education and literacy. There are abundant supplies of sutras in both classical Chinese and modern Chinese. However, there is still a distance between reading the sutras and practicing the teachings conveyed in them. Being able to memorize the sutras without comprehending the text is as futile as reading books but not understanding the message contained in them. To sum up, we will benefit from the sutras only if we practice what we have learned from them.

IT IS DIFFICULT
TO BE CONTEMPORARY WITH THE BUDDHA

A Chinese saying is often heard: "Which is the way home in the endless sea of humanity?" This means that a person is lost and without direction and cannot find refuge in his heart. In one sutra there is a metaphor: "A one-eyed turtle happens upon a hole in a piece of wood." There is a piece of wood with a hole in the middle of it floating in the vast seas, and there is a one-eyed turtle that surfaces from the ocean once every one thousand years. As it emerges from the deep seas, its head goes right through the hole in the wood. Imagine what a rare coincidence this is! In life, our chances of finding a real refuge for our souls is just as rare.

The Buddha said, "It is difficult to be contemporary with the Buddha." Although all living beings are ceaselessly reborn through the cycle of reincarnation into the Six Destinies of heaven, human, Asura [a pugnacious person], animal, hungry ghost and hell, we are rarely born as human beings. It is even more difficult to be born as a human at the same time that the Buddha is in this world. What is rarest of all is to be born human, live in the same age as the Buddha, and be able to meet him personally.

Sakyamuni Buddha was born more than two thousand years ago in India. Could we have been living in that same era? And if so, in such a large world, could we have been born in the same place as the Buddha? Even if these two conditions were met, it would still be unlikely that we would be able to see the Buddha at all. Therefore, it is difficult to be contemporary with the Buddha.

REPLACE MY OWN HEART WITH THE BUDDHA'S HEART

Although the Buddha's time dates back more than two thousand years before ours, if we can cultivate ourselves by following the instructions he left with us, we will be able to enter into his spirit. So long as we keep the Buddha in our hearts, it will be as if we were born in his time. However, even if we were living in the same place as the Buddha, if we heard his teachings but did not apply them well, we would still be far away from him.

It is recorded in the sutras that the Buddha once went to a small town with a population of ninety thousand. One third of the population met the Buddha and heard his lectures, one third heard that the Buddha was in town but did not see him, and the remaining one third not only did not see the Buddha, but never even heard of him. So how could they have learned Buddhism? This shows that even if one lives in the same age as the Buddha, it can still be hard to see the Buddha at all. In that small town, only one third of the people heard the Buddha lecture. What about us, born more than two thousand years later?

One third of the townspeople in the story never even heard of the Buddha. They were born in the same age as the Buddha but lived as if they were not, so how could they ever have learned the Buddha's dharma? One third heard of the Buddha but did not attend his lectures. What good did that do? The remaining one third saw the Buddha, but were they really able to comprehend and take his teachings to heart? After sifting through these townspeople, how many remained who were truly able to understand the Buddha's teachings? This shows that as long as people are able to receive and accept the Buddha's teachings, they will benefit from them, regardless of whether they are contemporary with the Buddha or not.

The Buddha told us, "For the buddhas of the past, present, and the future, mind alone creates everything." If we always chant the Buddha's name in our mind and replace our own heart with his heart, we will not only be contemporary with the Buddha, but will also be able to inspire our innate buddha-nature and become mediums that demonstrate the Buddha's wisdom. I often say that we must not belittle ourselves, because the Buddha is within our minds all the time. If we apply Buddhist mind and conduct to our daily lives, it will then be as if the Buddha himself were guiding us along. What difficulty is there then in becoming a contemporary of the Buddha?

CULTIVATE OURSELVES ACCORDING TO THE DHARMA AND APPLY IT WISELY

Modern people who admire the sages will search hard for a good mentor. But it is not easy to find a truly learned and virtuous person, since not everyone can have such qualities. The Buddha had both. We have learned a lot about the way he taught, and we also know many events that took place in his life. If we can carry out the lessons that we have read and heard, then the Buddha will always be present in our minds and our daily activities. Although it is difficult to be born at the same time as the Buddha, as long as we carry a Buddhist mind within us, it will be just as if we were living in the same age as the Buddha.

In the previous chapter, we talked about the difficulty of reading Buddhist sutras. Is it really difficult for us to read and comprehend Buddhist sutras? Not in this modern time of ours. Lectures on Buddhism are given everywhere and are often big events. Audiences can reach thousands, sometimes tens of thousands. Yet how many of these eager listeners can really bear the Buddhist dharma in mind and put it into practice? If everyone who heard the Buddhist sutras could apply the teachings conveyed in them to their daily lives, then our society would long since have been purified! Unfortunately, most people do not practice what they hear. What difference, then, is there between people who have and have not heard the teachings?

Nowadays, we generally enjoy a higher level of education and reading the sutras is less difficult than before. If we read the sutras and cultivate ourselves accordingly and use them as guidance in our daily lives, then everything we see will be the Buddha's deeds, and everything we hear will be the Buddha's words. Why then should it be difficult for us to live as if we were contemporary with the Buddha? Alas, our society has deviated far from the right doctrines and it seems that all the saints and sages are worlds away from us. It is not easy for people to learn the dharma.

WITH JUST ONE THOUGHT WE CAN LEARN THE BUDDHA'S TEACHINGS

The Buddha often said, "It may be eons before one has the chance to learn the dharma." But he also said, "In an instant, one can learn the dharma," meaning that learning the dharma is all in the mind. Is there not a big difference between an instant and eons? If we do not face the truth conveyed through the Buddhist teachings and put it into practice, it makes no difference whether or not we are born contemporary with the Buddha. On the contrary, even though we are separated by thousands of years from the Buddha, if we can cherish and abide by his philosophy, act and speak in our daily lives as he would, and have a heart like his, then what is gained in even an instant is the truth that the Buddha taught.

We do not have to be of a certain age or in a specific environment to learn the truth and comprehend it. Once when I attended a meeting at the Tzu Chi Junior College of Nursing, I heard a member of the Yi Te Mother/Sister

Association [formed of Tzu Chi commissioners who have been chosen to advise the students] say that on her way home on Sunday, she met some of our nursing students on the bus and asked them where they were returning from. "From spreading seeds of the Tzu Chi spirit," they answered her. "We went on a hiking trip held by the China Youth Corps with students from other schools. During this trip, we discovered that everybody really looks up to Tzu Chi students. Our behavior, speech and actions received a lot of positive comments. Now we know what an honor it is to be Tzu Chi students. In our conversations, we all took the chance to explain to others the spirit of kindness, compassion, joy and unselfish giving. We also told them what the Master told us—that we should humble ourselves and broaden our minds to care for others. Everyone liked us, because we were spreading great love, a pure, undefiled love."

Just imagine, these were students who had only been in Tzu Chi College for four months, but they were already able to practice the Buddhist spirit of kindness, compassion, joy and unselfish giving. Even when they were with students from other schools, they represented the image of Tzu Chi and were able to sow the seeds of the Tzu Chi spirit. Though young, they have been exposed to the Buddha's teachings because they attend our nursing college. In class, they learn professional skills, but they have naturally been influenced by the spirit of Tzu Chi and Buddhism. In so little time, they have evolved into young women who earn the respect of other people. If we have the desire to learn and earnestly accept the Buddha's teachings, then our mind will blend with the Buddha's. This is what is meant by "With just one thought, we can learn the Buddha's teachings."

It does not matter how much time we spend on learning the dharma. Once our minds have departed from that of the Buddha, it is difficult for us to be in contact with it again. If we can unite our minds with that of the Buddha, we can see him and learn his teachings in a split second. So I do not think it is so difficult to be contemporary with the Buddha. As long as we concentrate, we can learn the dharma in an instant. It's all in the mind: those who really want to learn Buddhism must really put their hearts into it, and when they learn the dharma, they must absorb it and then keep it in their minds and practice it in their daily conduct. Thus, it is not difficult at all to learn the Buddhist teachings.

IT IS DIFFICULT
TO CONTROL SENSUAL DESIRE

T he sixth difficulty to attaining buddhahood is "It is difficult to control sensual desire." "Sensual desire" seems to denote sexual desire, but in fact it is here used in a wider sense. "Sensual" refers to anything that has form and body. Anything that the eyes can see or the body can feel is sensual.

It Is Difficult Not to Take What You Want

To "control" our sensual desire means to control our minds. For example, when we see something very beautiful but are not able to control our minds, our natural reaction is to want to have it and we will try to take it. Some people take things rightfully, some do not. Although obtaining something rightfully involves the cheerful giving of other people, it actually stems from our desire for something we fancy and the consequent act of trying to obtain it. On the other hand, some people desire things that are not meant to be theirs. They are aware that it is wrong to want them, but cannot control the desire to do so. And so these people will break the precepts or violate the law. This is the kind of situation that arises when one cannot control one's sensual desire.

I remember a sad story that happened years ago. There was a young woman who lived in a happy family and was loved dearly by her mother. Later the young woman fell in love and got married, and her mother provided a generous dowry.

The husband, a civil servant, was not as well-off as his wife's family and he lived in a rented apartment. After they were married, the young wife still expected to have her accustomed luxuries and could not get used to their tight financial situation. She constantly complained to her husband that she was ashamed of their living conditions. She hoped that he would soon buy a beautiful home, but he could not afford one. She regularly went back to her mother, who agreed to all her requests and gave her whatever she wanted.

The husband was a law-abiding and down-to-earth person, and every month he gave his entire salary to his wife. Although they lived frugally, they still could not save up enough money to buy a place of their own. It galled her to think that other people owned their own homes while hers was rented. Even though she did not have enough money, she constantly went to look at houses for sale.

A FAMILY RUINED BY DESIRE

For years, the woman would go to her mother with plans of buying an apartment.

"I saw an apartment that is selling for about NT$2 million [US$62,500]. I plan to buy it."

Her mother asked her, "How much money do you have?"

"Around two hundred thousand."

Her mother tried to persuade her to change her mind, but it was to no avail.

Sometimes she talked to her husband about buying an apartment. "I saw an apartment today that costs around one million."

"How much money do we have in savings now?"

"Around two hundred thousand."

Hearing this amount, the husband gently tried to talk her out of the idea of owning their own apartment.

However, for more than ten years, she bustled around looking at homes, hoping to buy one. Whenever a new apartment building was completed, she would go look at it. She always wanted to buy one, but it was always beyond her means.

Twelve years into her marriage, she saw a unit in Taipei that cost NT$3.8 million. It was very attractive indeed, and she wanted it so much that she almost went insane. She went to her mother every day and nagged her to lend her two million.

Her mother said, "I don't have any problem with lending you the money, but where are you going to get the rest of the money?"

"I can borrow it from someone else."

Her mother asked pointedly, "And do you have enough money to make the monthly payments?"

In fact, her mother knew that the husband's salary would never be enough to pay the mortgage. So her mother said to her, "Calm down now and don't be so obsessed with this idea."

However, she was unable to control her desire. She even blamed her mother for not being willing to help her, and she broke off all relations with her.

After she severed ties with her family, she still could not curb her desire. She turned and vented her anger on her husband. Every day she nagged him for being useless and unable to give her what she wanted. Goaded by her constant badgering and at his wit's end, the husband began to accept bribes. But before he could pocket the money, he was caught and sentenced to jail.

After paying such a high price, did her desire finally die out? No, it became worse. She even made her children shoplift goods from department stores. One day her son was caught red-handed stealing some expensive pens in a bookstore, and he was sent to a juvenile detention home. The woman was left with only a thirteen-year-old daughter by her side. But by now she seemed to have become mentally disturbed and often scolded and mistreated her daughter. One day after school, the daughter was walking along the street crying, obviously depressed. She was hit by a car and was killed instantly. In the end, the woman had nothing left in the world and suffered a nervous breakdown.

This tragedy involved the whole family. The woman's irrational desires caused the death of her own daughter. To satisfy her craving, her husband did something very foolish and was put behind bars for years. She led her son to steal, and he ended up in a detention home. Finally, she herself became mentally deranged. All of this was caused by her inability to control the desires of her senses!

Therefore, the Buddha said to us, "It is difficult to control sensual desire." How many lives and families have been ruined because of uncontrolled desire?

HAPPINESS LIES IN CONTENTMENT

The Buddha taught us to have correct views about material things and worldly passions. If we can learn the truth and be reasonable, we will have proper concepts regarding the taking and giving of things. We can take things we are entitled to have, and give generously to others what we have in abundance. On the other hand, we should not desire things that we don't deserve to have. If we have control over our minds, we will not make mistakes.

Many people do things that they regret their whole lives because they cannot control sensual desire. One single wrong thought will lead to a series of mistakes, so we must be careful at all times.

IT IS DIFFICULT
NOT TO PURSUE FINE THINGS

E very person has desires. In the previous chapter, I talked about the difficulty of controlling sensual desires because the world is full of all sorts of material things that tempt us and lead us into confusion. Therefore the Buddha also said, "It is difficult not to pursue fine things."

Human beings are always in pursuit of something. If we consider something to be worth it, we will ceaselessly search for it. Most people do this all the time. However, these endless pursuits are also the cause of many of our worries. Many people have wrecked their futures because of the urge to fulfill their cravings.

People with strong desires are never satisfied with their current situation and always feel empty and lost. Because they are dissatisfied with what they have, they are constantly in quest of something else. In the course of pursuing their goals, they eventually lose sight of their true nature. To help people break free from their endless desires, the Buddha used all sorts of methods to teach his followers to heed his admonitions.

The Buddha often said, "Life is impermanent, and everything is a dream or a bubble." Unfortunately, human beings are ignorant and impractical. They either think that everything is void in the world so that they do not need to strive after anything meaningful, or cling to what they have and never stop chasing after more. To liberate people from such incessant pursuit, the Buddha used his unprejudiced wisdom to teach people of all levels.

ENDLESS PURSUIT WILL NOT BRING PEACE OF MIND

In the Buddha's time, the king of a small kingdom was the richest man in the world. As a devout Brahman, he deeply believed that the prestige and power he enjoyed in his present life resulted from the good deeds he performed in his past life. Therefore, he endeavored to cultivate blessings for his next life by giving generously.

One day the king opened the doors to his treasure house and announced, "For the next seven days, people from anywhere and of any race can come to me and ask for help. I will not turn anyone down." He divided his treasure into numerous piles, each pile the size of sixty dates gathered together. Each person that came received one pile. Although many people came, there was still a lot of treasure left near the end of the seven-day term.

The Buddha knew of the king's generous deed.

71

But the Buddha also knew that the king's magnanimity did not originate from true enlightenment, because he was still motivated by the desire for something—good fortune in his next life.

The Buddha disguised himself as a Brahman mendicant and approached the king. The king said to him, "Come, tell me all your difficulties and I will grant you anything you need."

"I know Your Majesty wishes to give generously in order to cultivate blessings," the mendicant said, "so I am here to seek a portion of your treasure."

The king said, "Alright then, you can take a pile."

The mendicant took a pile and started to leave. But after taking only seven steps, he returned and put the treasure back.

The king, surprised, asked, "Why are you putting it back?"

"Originally, I would have been happy with three meals to eat each day," the mendicant answered. "Now, with all this treasure, I feel insecure living this vagabond lifestyle, so I would really like to have a house of my own."

The king considered this a reasonable request, so

he said, "Then take another pile."

The mendicant took another pile, but after a few steps he returned again and put the pile back.

The king inquired, "Is something the matter?"

"I was thinking: with the money I get from selling the treasure, I would only be able to build a house, but I still wouldn't have enough to get married."

"Fine, take three piles. That should be enough for you to build a house and marry yourself a wife."

So the mendicant took three piles and turned to go. Once again, he went as far as seven steps, went back, and replaced the treasure. Quite amazed, the king said, "You are a very curious person—aren't three piles enough for you?"

"After doing some thinking, I don't reckon they will be enough. Even after I build my house, get married and have children, I will still need money to hire servants for my wife and children, or to furnish the house more comfortably, so these treasures are not enough."

Even with someone like this mendicant, the king was quite tolerant. "Then take seven piles."

The mendicant took seven piles and walked for a

distance, but then he returned again and put everything back.

"You are really a strange person," the king said angrily. "Aren't you happy with enough treasure to build a house, get married and hire servants? There is enough to last you a lifetime!"

The mendicant sighed. "No matter how I figure it, I still feel there is not enough. Even if I myself have everything, my son will need to get married when he grows up. Alas, in our lives there are too many things to pursue and too many things to do. Besides, life is impermanent and I would rather live my life as it is now: simple and easy, without the mental burden of guarding over my fortune or worrying about my family. In this way, I can live quietly and peacefully for the rest of my life. Therefore, I think my present lifestyle is the most ideal and carefree."

"That's very true," the king suddenly realized. "There is no end to the things we chase after in life. My life is very good now, but I still want to pursue blessings for my future life. If I keep on chasing blessings life after life, I will never be really free. As a king, I have to worry about my people and national affairs, and I also have to protect my country from the aggressions of other nations. Is this really good fortune? I ought to be seeking a freer and more transcendent life!"

The Buddha knew what the king was thinking. "There is now an enlightened person, the Buddha, in this world. If I were looking for riches, I would rather follow the Buddha, because he has a boundless wealth of wisdom which can make me free and unencumbered. I think it would be better for me to pursue the truth that the Buddha preaches." Murmuring this as if to himself, the Buddha walked away, leaving the king behind.

When the king heard that there was an enlightened person in this world, he suddenly remembered. "That's right! My people have been saying that Prince Siddhartha has become the Buddha and he is now the teacher of all people. So why don't I go to the Buddha to ask him to enlighten me and accept me as his disciple?" Straightaway, he called for a horse and rode to the Abode of the Jetavana Garden.

When the king saw the Buddha, it was like seeing an old friend. He wondered where he had met the Buddha before. The Buddha smiled at him and said, "It's been such a short time since we parted and already you don't recognize me?" As the king looked into the Buddha's benevolent face, the truth dawned on him. He prostrated himself and thanked the Buddha for enlightening him.

The Buddha was good at creating the most opportune circumstances to impart his wisdom to people. In this instance, the Buddha disguised himself as a Brahman mendicant to approach the king, provoked the king by repeatedly asking for and then returning the treasure, prompted the king to examine his life and conduct, and finally led the king to enlightenment. Such is the wise guidance of the Buddha.

ABANDONING DESIRE LEADS TO PEACE OF MIND AND FREEDOM

The Buddha often said, "In life we never stop wanting," and he therefore observed that "It is difficult not to pursue fine things." Take the king in the story for example: he was the ruler of a nation and the wealthiest person in the world, but he still felt that he had to pursue good fortune for the next life. The Brahman mendicant (representative of all people) wanted to build a house, wed a wife and have servants. He even had to worry about the well-being of his descendants. This example clearly demonstrates how burdensome life becomes because there is no end to wanting.

Of course, "wanting" is not always bad. While we are learning Buddhism, we "want" to improve and cultivate ourselves. We cultivate ourselves to free our minds, to fight the temptations of sensual desire, and to finally reach an unburdened, peaceful state without desire or greed.

NOT TO GET ANGRY WHEN INSULTED

The eighth difficulty in attaining buddhahood is, "It is difficult not to get angry when insulted." When people are angry, they tend to say, "I can't stand it anymore!" What can't they stand? Usually it is having been bullied, taken advantage of or treated unreasonably. These are the situations that usually cause people to lose their temper.

Why do people fail to be tolerant? This is due to the three negative sentiments of greed, anger and delusion common to all people. These three negative sentiments cause people to feel offended whenever someone takes a little advantage of them and breed intolerance between family members and strife in society. Thus, a life that could have been so wonderful is instead full of discord.

ENDURING HUNGER AND RESOLVING HATRED WITH VIRTUE

The Buddha became who he was because he was able to suffer attacks and insults that no one else could and accomplish tasks that no one else was able to. That was how he became a buddha.

When the Buddha was still alive, there was in his congregation a monk by the name of Devadatta, who was also the Buddha's cousin. Devadatta was aggressively ambitious and wanted to replace the Buddha as leader of the sangha. He therefore got in with Ajatasatru, the crown prince of the kingdom of Magadha [where the Buddha then resided], who wished to hasten his own ascent to the throne then held by his father. Following a scheme that Devadatta devised, Ajatasatru usurped the throne, jailed his father, and prohibited anyone from giving him food or water. While Ajatasatru was trying to starve his own father to death, Devadatta was also plotting against the Buddha's life.

One day, Devadatta and King Ajatasatru announced that no one in the city where the Buddha and his followers lived was to give them alms. Anyone who disobeyed would be severely punished. Therefore, no one in the city dared to offer food to the Buddha and the monks.

Although the Buddha and his disciples ate only one meal at noon every day, it was the meal they relied on for subsistence. As the days dragged on, it became difficult for the sangha to hold out. So the Buddha told Maudgalyayana, Sariputra, Kasyapa, and other chief disciples to lead the majority of the monks to other places, while only the Buddha, Ananda and five hundred monks remained in the city. They suffered hunger in the hope of moving the king with their endurance.

Compassion Subdues Wild Elephants

When Devadatta heard that the Buddha's chief disciples had left the city with most of the monks, he said to Ajatasatru, "Now that only the Buddha, Ananda and five hundred monks have stayed behind, we can use this opportunity to destroy them."

Devadatta urged the king to invite the Buddha and his assembly to the palace for a banquet. His plot was to intoxicate five hundred elephants and then set them loose on the path of the Buddha and his monks. Elephants are very powerful animals, and when they are drunk they become violent and attack anyone in their path. After Devadatta and the king had devised their plan, the king proceeded to invite the Buddha to the palace for the meal.

Although the Buddha was well aware of their scheme, he still accepted the invitation with delight.

When he and the monks were halfway to the palace, the wild elephants suddenly dashed out of nowhere. All the onlookers were horrified and ran for their lives. Only the Buddha, Ananda and the monks stood still. Even as the drunken elephants rushed towards them, the Buddha stood motionless.

Oddly, having created such a commotion, these wild, clamoring elephants suddenly became gentle and subdued before the Buddha and the assembly, and they knelt down as if prostrating themselves before the Buddha. The Buddha smiled serenely and patted some of the elephants, then he walked through them and entered the palace.

Ajatasatru was stunned by what he saw. He realized that the Buddha had the dignity and power not only to humble people, but even to pacify drunk, wild elephants. With awe and reverence swelling in his heart, Ajatasatru respectfully offered the meal to the Buddha and the sangha. The Buddha was not angered by the staged "accident," nor did he bear any grudge against Ajatasatru, to whom he sincerely gave his blessings after the meal. Such was the Buddha's great virtue of endurance.

Ordinary people will fight to the end for the smallest mistreatment, but not the Buddha. Although he was insulted, harassed, starved and almost murdered, he still remained absolutely calm and harbored no grudge. From this instance, we can see that the Buddha had a mind as pure as a clear mirror, a heart where no anger or hatred but only boundless love abided.

Love, compassion and forgiveness can replace anger and hatred. When a person has love, compassion and forgiveness in his heart, how can there be room for anger to exist? And if we can eliminate anger, how can there be any strife?

Probably many people have had the following experience: sitting indoors while it rains outside, you can feel the chill just by listening to the rain fall even though there is no cold wind coming in. In this case, the sensation is the result of mental activity. The Buddha repeatedly reminded us that "Mind alone creates everything." Whether it is how you treat other people or vice versa, everything that you do or feel is dictated solely by your mind. It is the same for all living beings.

The Buddha said, "It is difficult not to get angry when insulted," meaning that it is truly rare for a person not to be at all offended when he is humiliated. If a person is not the least bit bothered when other people show contempt for him, that would be something truly remarkable. How many people like this can be found in this world?

Many people drive themselves up a blind alley by thinking too much. Maybe no one did them any harm or had any disrespect for them, but if they keep suspecting others of the worst intentions, they will be tormented by their own suspicions.

Confucius once said that if people had the ability to endure insults, there would be no contention in the world. This worldly saint and the otherworldly saint, the Buddha, apparently taught people the same thing— to endure insults.

BE CALM AND WIN WITHOUT FIGHTING

In the Chou dynasty [1122–249 BC] in ancient China, a person named Chi Sheng-tzu specialized in raising fighting cocks. When two fighting cocks confront each other, the reaction of one to the slightest movement of the other is instantaneous. A fierce fight then ensues, sometimes causing both cocks to become wounded and covered with blood. But they will keep fighting until either both are critically injured or one is dead.

Emperor Hsuan enjoyed watching cockfights, so Chi raised and trained fighting cocks for him. One day, someone brought a strong fighting cock to the emperor, who handed it over to Chi. A few days later, the emperor asked him, "So, is the new cock ready to fight now?"

Chi replied, "Not yet, because it still has the impulse to fight, so it is not ready yet."

Another few days went by and the emperor put the same question to Chi. "Not yet," Chi answered, "because it gets excited when it catches a glimpse of other cocks."

Days later the emperor asked again. Chi replied, "It is ready now, because it does not move at all when it sees other cocks or hears their squawks. Like a wooden chicken, it is no longer affected by what happens around it. Therefore it is now ready to fight."

This must seem like a strange theory to you, right? Isn't fighting all about being impulsive and ready to fight in order to win? This is what we normally assume. Chi thought that although the cock was very strong and combative, if it was provoked to attack first by the slightest movement, it would certainly lose a fight. Therefore, he trained the chicken to hold back its impulse to fight before actually beginning to fight.

Later, when this cock entered the arena, it would simply stand fixedly. No matter how its opponent tried to provoke it, it stood as motionless and unperturbed as a wooden chicken. It merely stared steadily at its opponent, invoking fear with its inscrutability and causing the opponent to back out of the fight. Even animals employ psychological tactics, not to mention human beings!

As human beings, we must have the capability of remaining calm, and must not feel insecure all the time thinking that everyone is hostile to us. We must treat other people with forbearance and refrain from thinking that we will look foolish if we don't contend with others. A Chinese saying tells us that "Great wisdom takes on the appearance of foolishness." Do not worry when other people laugh at you for being foolish. Beware instead of people considering you too smart, for too smart means "cunning." If we hear comments such as, "How can he be so foolish? He allows other people to take advantage of him and does not care at all," we should hope that we are the person referred to.

I am sickened every time I watch the news. From legislators to the mob, violence seems to be their platform and fist fights the resolution of all problems. Our lives could actually be wonderful, but why have they become such an ugly struggle? The reason lies in the unwillingness to be patient and to make concessions.

In the previous chapter I talked about, "It is difficult not to pursue fine things." Wealthy people long for more wealth and people of high social status seek more power. That is why discordance and chaos come to exist. If we carry out our duties earnestly and make the Buddha's mind our own mind, there will be no more strife. Students of Buddhism must strive to achieve the ideal of remaining unperturbed when insulted, a sign of true spiritual cultivation.

ENDURANCE MAKES EVERYTHING EASY

The Buddha told us, "It is difficult not to get angry when insulted." We say that spiritual cultivation is not difficult if we have resolution, but it is indeed difficult to develop complete endurance. Learning Buddhism is learning endurance. If we fail to endure the most trivial matters, life will become very tough to live. Spiritual cultivation without endurance is simply not spiritual cultivation anymore.

I hope all of you can remember the lesson of the fighting cock: be still, do not act rashly and no one will harass you. If through spiritual cultivation we can reach a state of inner tranquillity, all difficulties in the world can naturally be resolved.

In learning Buddhism, one of the goals we must achieve is an imperturbable inner world that is tolerant and unaffected by the external world. Without an imperturbable mind, for example, if you are meditating in a sanctuary while it rains outside, the weather can make you very restless. You might think, "Wouldn't it be more comfortable to be tucked in bed under a warm comforter in such cold weather? Why should I be sitting here?" If we fail to coexist peacefully with nature, we will fail to achieve a state of imperturbability. In our daily lives, we must also remember to remain uninfluenced by people and to be tolerant and accommodating. By so doing, we should be able to prevent discord and strife.

IT IS DIFFICULT
NOT TO TAKE ADVANTAGE
OF HIGH POSITION

The cold winter winds intensify the bitter chill. I hear that days ago snow began to fall on the mountaintops, forming a blanket of white. Even in the populated flatlands, the cold, aggravated by the incessant drizzle, is piercing.

Normally it is colder in the mountains than in the flatlands, but many people head for the frozen mountains as soon as they have a day off. Reports of accidents don't stop people from hiking in the mountains. This is the obduracy of ordinary people: they do not appreciate the beauty nearest them, but instead always chase after things and sights elsewhere. Such is the perverseness and stubbornness of ordinary people.

The eighth difficulty in attaining buddhahood is "It is difficult not to get angry when insulted," which means that it is hard not to get upset when someone looks down on us. The Buddha then went on to talk about the difficulty of not looking down on people, not feeling superior, or not taking advantage when one is in the position to do so. Human beings always strive upward and seek more commanding positions, yet not many people can refrain from being arrogant or flaunting high positions once they have attained them. This is the reason the Buddha said, "It is difficult not to take advantage of high position."

To the Great Mind, Fame and Wealth Are Disposable

Look at society now. In the newspaper, everything we read is somehow connected to power, fame, or wealth. On television, all we see are government officials and legislators fighting and hurling insults at one another. We see legislators jumping and fighting on top of the podium, which should be sacred. And what for? To gain a good position. The higher the position, the greater the power. Therefore, it is difficult for people not to go after power and position. These are the actions of common, vulgar people. Only those who are above the mundane pursuits of this world, who aspire to the level of sages and saints, can look beyond fame and wealth.

Sakyamuni Buddha was originally the crown prince of a kingdom, but he gave up the power, position and wealth of a king and sought the truth of human life. To a man with superhuman wisdom, worldly power and wealth are like worn-out shoes that are not worth pursuing and are easily discarded. However, common people do not feel this way and are therefore plagued with worries.

The Buddha had extraordinary wisdom and saw wealth as floating clouds and power as worn-out shoes. Is this a state that only the Buddha can attain? Not necessarily. Even an ordinary person can also achieve the Buddha's state of mind if he can look beyond the things within his immediate vision.

GREATNESS IN HUMILITY

Once when I was in Taipei, I was really moved by a young couple who came to see me. The wife was petite and simply dressed. Despite the cold weather she was thinly clad, with jeans that were clean but looked well-worn. She held out a soda can to me-her hands were rough, evidently those of a laborer. Unsuspecting, I took the can and almost dropped it from its weight. How could such a small can weigh so much? What was in it?

The wife kept saying, "Master, please accept this can. Master, will you please accept it?"

I opened the can and found a plastic bag inside, in which were nine small gold ingots and some gold coins and necklaces wrapped in paper. She piously knelt on the ground and kept entreating me to accept her donation. Looking at her, obviously not dressed warmly enough for the cold weather, I was full of gratitude but also a little doubtful.

"Why are you donating so much gold, and how did you come to have it?" I asked.

She said, "Most of it my father gave me, some I bought only last year."

"What do you do for a living?"

"I work as a seamstress at a garment factory."

Her husband also worked in the same factory, and the two of them shared one goal: to contribute what they could for the construction of the Tzu Chi Hospital. As long as they were healthy, had work and could make ends meet, they felt that what spare money they had would be put to better use in my hands, because my goal of establishing a hospital was a meaningful mission that would have long-term effects. "We have no use for this stuff," the wife said. "It is all quite the same to us whether we have it or not."

They were an ordinary couple, but they had an extraordinary wish-to donate all of their savings for a hospital that would save lives. I could tell that their financial condition was just average, yet with their rough hands they gave away those costly gold ingots, coins and necklaces. The gold was valuable, but that value could hardly compare to the beauty and goodness in the couple's hearts. Their sincere wish to help people was truly touching.

This couple could have sold the gold to pay their daily expenses or buy prettier and warmer clothes. However, they did not even think of keeping themselves warmer, let alone getting more than they already had. Thus, if one's considerations transcend worldly material things, it will not be difficult to refrain from taking advantage of one's position.

In August 1999, members of the Tzu Chi Foundation went onto the streets to raise funds for earthquake victims in Turkey. Throughout this activity, I witnessed many incidents that proved that ordinary people can be just as great as the Buddha.

One example is Wu Tung-hsien, president of the Shinkong syndicate and a Tzu Chi Honorary Board member, who regularly donates money to sponsor the Tzu Chi charity mission. This time, to help disaster victims in Turkey, Mr. Wu not only donated a large sum of money himself but also went bravely onto the streets. Why do I say bravely? Because the site where Mr. Wu conducted his fund-raising was nowhere else but in front of the Shinkong Building, headquarters of the Shinkong group. Imagine the president of a huge corporation, standing before the building he owned, bowing humbly to a crowd that might have included his employees. To help suffering people in a distant land, he braved the scorching sun and patiently explained to strangers the purpose of the fund-raising. This takes determination and courage.

With his wealth and power, Mr. Wu really didn't have to go through so much trouble. He could have stayed in a comfortably air-conditioned office and ordered his employees to do the hard work. Or he could have thought rightfully that since he had already made a generous donation, there was no need for him to stand on the streets raising funds at the speed of only one or ten dollars at a time. If he said that a man in his position did not have to humble himself like that, it could only be called human nature. But he didn't use any of these advantages or excuses. Instead, to help people, he was able to let go of all that and personally devote himself to practicing good deeds. This is what I call "not taking advantage of high position."

Another example is the superintendent of the Tzu Chi General Hospital in Hualien, Chen Ying-ho. Even though he was a superintendent [a profession highly esteemed in Taiwan] and the head of the only major medical center in eastern Taiwan, Dr. Chen also went onto the streets. Because it was his first time, he was naturally a little intimidated by the prospect of opening his mouth to total strangers. So he "hid" at the side of the road, and emerged only when he saw someone coming. When I witnessed the scene, I was truly moved. I was moved that Dr. Chen did not feel superior because of what he had already achieved, moved that he was able to cast away the aura of authority belonging to the head of a major hospital, and moved that he was able to humble himself for the selfless cause of charity.

These two gentlemen, with their position and power, could well have pursued their own interests or ordered other people to do the hard work. But they didn't. All they wanted was to do their best to help others. They proved that with a mind that looks beyond worldly concerns, it is very easy not to take advantage of high position.

In this world, there are many people who are wealthy and powerful, but not many have minds that are free of worldly pursuits. That was why the Buddha told us, "It is difficult not to take advantage of high position." But he also said, "Mind alone creates everything." If you have the will, you can surpass the temptations of wealth, power and fame. People learning Buddhism must make an example of these two gentlemen. If we see people fighting over power or fame, then we must remind ourselves not to be like them.

IT IS DIFFICULT
TO MAINTAIN A SIMPLE MIND

S tepping out of my room, I see the first faint light of morning at the horizon. I open the doors to the main sanctuary and enter. The light is off and the darkness inside intensifies the quiet atmosphere. I prostrate myself before the statue of the Buddha, sit down and adjust my posture, after which the nuns chant the sutras and then meditate. In the sky, the first faint light has been replaced by a silver white stripe and I can sense that dawn is near, so I close my eyes, my mind as quiet as the atmosphere. When I open my eyes again, I see that it is already bright outside.

Time flows on like a river, unnoticed. Between every daybreak and sunset, we live out our busy days. Although we never escape our external surroundings, we never really pay attention to the changes in them. In everyday life, there are many things that we do not pay much attention to, things that simply pass by.

CHERISH THE SIMPLE LIFE

When the Buddha told us, "It is difficult to maintain a simple mind," he wanted us to know that life is meant to be simple and free. It is in our unen-

lightened state that life becomes complicated and full
of worry and agony. We all know the old Chinese saying: "There was originally no trouble in the world—it
is fools who stir up trouble for themselves." Yet in
life, we are always troubling ourselves with people
and events. Time ticks away, but our thoughts brood
over the troubles of the past. This is the worrying
mind of the ordinary person that the Buddha was
thinking of when he said, "It is difficult to maintain a
simple mind."

Why do so many people spend their days in dis-
quietude? Because with a complicated mind, they
make comparisons and distinctions. For example, they
feel that they do a lot more work than others do and
become arrogant. Or they think that other people's
hard work is not so important and their own minimal
work as nothing to be embarrassed about. Either situation causes agitation.

Our work must be based on our ability. If we have
so much strength, we will do so much work. If we really know ourselves, then we will not constantly compare ourselves with other people and create worries for
ourselves.

JOY AND SERENITY COME FROM A HEART THAT DOES NOT COMPARE

There is a story in *Chuang-Tzu* [a book of parables and allegories attributed to the Chinese Taoist philosopher of that name]. A huge fish that was several miles long had lived in the North Sea for thousands of years. One day there suddenly came a whirlwind that scooped up the fish and transformed it into a roc, a bird of great size and strength. When it spread its wings and sailed the winds, it could soar high up into the sky. The roc set out to fly from the North Sea to the South Sea, a journey that would take half a year to complete. It flew without stopping. When it looked down, it saw white clouds that looked like horses traversing the skies; when it looked up, there was the gray, limitless sky and nothing else. After six months of continuous flying, the roc finally reached the South Sea.

On the ground, there was a sparrow. When it saw the huge bird in the sky, it thought, "Why should it fly so high? Even with its great size, it must fly very hard to complete its journey. I am small and light and can fly effortlessly. Any little branch can be my resting spot. If I want to fly higher but am unable to, I can simply land on the ground. My life is free and easy. There is nothing extraordinary about the roc."

This is only a parable. Whether the great bird really exists is not important. What we must explore is the sparrow's act of comparing itself with the roc. Is the sparrow really freer? In fact, the sparrow, being too small and too weak to fly as high as the huge bird, was consoling itself by disparaging the roc—the sour grapes mentality at work.

Actually, with its large body and wings that extended for miles, where else was the roc to fly except towards the high skies? The ability to fly high is something that comes naturally for the powerful roc, not something that it flaunts. Although the sparrow was small, there were advantages to being small too. Therefore, the sparrow did not need to compare itself with the magnificent bird, and the roc certainly did not need to envy the agility of the sparrow. In daily life, we should do what is within our capacity, let bygones be bygones, and refrain from hanging on to past events.

I often remind people around me to let go of troubling thoughts. When our thoughts dwell on past events, we are disquieted. If we ignore the present and look only to the future, then we are fantasizing. Therefore we must make the best use of the present moment and do the best we can.

Although we walk with our feet on the ground, our feet are never glued to the ground. We advance forward by pushing one foot against the ground, with the other foot raised behind in preparation. So we are constantly moving forward and never tread the same spot twice. Let us then not complicate our originally simple life by adhering pointlessly to past events and thoughts that ought to be left behind.

If we can return to our true nature, then maintaining a simple mind that is unaffected by external things around us is no longer difficult. Do not complicate simple matters, but instead try to simplify complicated matters. By so doing, our lives will be easy and peaceful. As a matter of fact, aren't we already living life quite heedless of external affairs? When I enter the main sanctuary in the morning, no one can see anyone else because the light is so dim.

And then when daylight breaks, everyone becomes visible. Yet who can still recall at what moment he or she sees the faces of the others? Isn't it true that we live quite unaware of what happens around us? Only when we maintain a simple mind can we really be free and at ease.

IT IS DIFFICULT
TO STUDY WIDELY AND THOROUGHLY

I t is difficult for a learner to study with total concentration, and even harder to study with both concentration and thoroughness. We can then imagine the difficulty of studying widely and thoroughly.

Most people only think about studying widely. There are so many things that they want to learn, but they are neither persistent nor able to study in depth. After learning just the basics of one subject, they already want to move on to another subject. Their minds are constantly changing and their efforts are scattered. They come up with something new every day but do nothing really well. There is a Chinese saying, "You learn ten things but are bad at nine," which means that we may study widely but lack the thoroughness to master even one subject.

It takes patience and concentration to accomplish anything we undertake. With patience, we can continue to learn, no matter how arduous it may be. With concentration, we can comprehend completely the truth of one subject, and with that the truths of all things. Yet the problem is that we often cannot concentrate, so we find that we cannot comprehend any discipline thoroughly.

VIEWING THE SKY THROUGH A BAMBOO TUBE

During the period of the Warring States (403–222 BC) in ancient China, there was a man who claimed he knew everything from past to present. He was always telling other people how he was well versed in the books, people and history of the past, and he could quote whole chapters. As for contemporary issues, he believed he also had a comprehensive understanding.

One day, he thought, "People all praise Chuang Tzu [the great Chinese Taoist philosopher] for being knowledgeable, but I am even more learned and nobody has ever heard of me."

Therefore, he decided to have a debate with Chuang Tzu to prove that he was the better of the two. He held his head high and arrogantly strode to the philosopher's residence, confident of his erudition. When he met Chuang Tzu, he started talking without pause about all the things he knew, but Chuang Tzu simply smiled and listened to him quietly. When the visitor finally finished talking, Chuang Tzu gently but seriously rebutted his flawed theories.

The arrogant person was quite stunned. He had imagined that he was the most extraordinary person in the world and knew everything there was to know, but he now realized that what he knew was merely superficial and rudimentary. It was Chuang Tzu, silent and dignified, who really possessed a deep understanding of the universe. After listening to the philosopher's succinct and subtle analyses, his arrogance was totally subdued. He realized that there was someone else who was more capable than he was.

Later, he related the event to a friend. "I was wrong. I originally thought of myself as very learned since I knew all these profound theories. Now I know that Chuang Tzu is the one whose knowledge is as profound as the deep sea!"

His friend laughed and said, "What a nerve you had to debate with Chuang Tzu! He is an intellectual giant with one foot in the sky and one foot on the ground and he knows this universe inside out. His knowledge is immeasurable. In fact, what you have seen of his learning is as if you were looking at the sky through a bamboo tube—you haven't seen the whole picture yet!"

After reading this story, we can also ask ourselves how much we have learned. How much do people who think they understand everything really know? The arrogant person in the story did in fact know quite a lot, but why was he still unable to compete with Chuang Tzu? It is because Chuang Tzu put his theories into practice. He lived simply and was spiritually content and free. From Chuang Tzu's book, *Hsiao Yao You (Joyful Journey)*, we can see how free and joyful his life was. The difference between the arrogant man and Chuang Tzu was that the former "learned," and the latter "learned and practiced what he learned."

PUT YOUR MIND TO IT

In learning Buddhism we should also do as Chuang Tzu did: practice what we learn. We all have the potential to lead lives that are as joyful and unburdened as his.

Once, two reporters asked me a question about maintaining a simple mind that is unaffected by external affairs. "Master, you told us not to think too much, but you also mentioned, 'please be mindful in doing your work.' Aren't these two statements contradictory?"

"When you have truly put your mind to what you are doing, you will not think much about it," I explained to them. "A while ago, you went with me to visit the construction site for the second phase of the Tzu Chi Hospital. You visited the third floor, the Still Thoughts Hall and the basement. While you were going up and down the stairs, did you ever pay attention to how you were walking?"

They replied, "No."

"Do you remember when you went to the rehabilitation department and saw the patients doing their exercises? You could tell that although they really wanted to, it was difficult for them to stand up. Some patients wanted to raise their hands, but they had to try extremely hard to do so. We usually walk without thinking about it, and we do just fine. Actually, we move so easily and naturally now because we learned diligently when we were small. This is what I mean when I say, 'When you have truly put your mind to what you are doing, you will not think much about it.' Healthy people can walk naturally without worrying, but people who are undergoing rehabilitation must put their minds to it all the time!"

All of us should be able to live joyful, carefree lives, but why are people so often plagued with worries? We worry when we see expressions that seem unfriendly or hear remarks that sound hostile. In fact, other people do not intend to make us worry, but we choose to carry their actions in our minds, which gives rise to all sorts of worries. If our thoughts constantly linger on things that happen around us, we will always be wondering if people are against us. We will be very unhappy.

"To learn" means to transform worries into wisdom and to progress from just having the intention to do something to putting one's mind to it. When we want to learn a lot—that is, we "have the intention" of doing it—it is not the same as "putting one's mind to it." Chuang Tzu focused tirelessly on his studies, and that is why he could learn thoroughly and make what he learned an integral part of his life and thought. This is how one's learning acquires depth.

As students of the Buddha, we need to learn with even more thoroughness. We must remember to study broadly, but what is equally important is to learn thoroughly. On the path of learning Buddhism, there are

115

many difficulties that we can only overcome with profound knowledge.

STUDYING THOROUGHLY BUT ALSO WIDELY

Unlike people in ancient times, many people in the modern age study thoroughly but not widely. Modern science and knowledge are very profound and specialized, so when people are studying at school, they have to choose the subject that interests them most and concentrate on it. Take for instance medicine, which is divided into many specialties. If you choose surgery, you have to study the textbooks and perform dissections before you can apply your skills on human bodies. With enough experience, you are then ready for clinical work. There are also many sub-divisions within the field of surgery, such as general surgery, chest surgery, plastic surgery, brain surgery, etc. If a person with a head injury goes to a general surgery department, the doctor will probably not accept the patient, because head injuries belong to the field of brain surgery. This shows that although doctors study very thoroughly, they are unable to study widely.

In the past, it used to be that people had to study everything, but not thoroughly. Now, like doctors, people must have a great deal of expertise in one area. Life is never as ideal as we would like it to be. Ordinary people want to learn everything but learn none of it well; professionals have very specialized knowledge that is not interchangeable.

In the case of religion, some people start by selecting a certain sect. Take for instance people learning Buddhism. Some choose the Pure Land sect, some choose the Meditative sect, and still others choose the Esoteric sect. Those studying the Pure Land sect chant the name of Amitabha, the Buddha of boundless light or life, and do not study Buddhist teachings, because they think words are useless. They feel that focusing on recitations is sufficient and see no need for meditation. Practitioners of the Meditative sect believe that through meditation they can eliminate evil thoughts and become buddhas by sudden enlightenment. They believe that they can be transformed into a new person through meditation, and that a state of complete oblivion to the external world can elevate them to the level of saints. Aside from these fundamental differences, each sect has different rules governing the reading of sutras or the method of prostration. As a result, many people may be experts in their own sect, but they do not go further to learn the comprehensive truth.

DIFFERENT RELIGIONS, SAME LOVING HEARTS

When people with different religions come together, it is natural that they have different views on certain matters. Some Buddhists discriminate against believers of other religions, because they think Buddhism is the supreme faith and the Buddha's great wisdom encompasses the truth of the universe. Believers of other religions might also discriminate against Buddhism or religions different from their own. Christians often believe that people who believe in God will be saved and those who don't will go to Hell. Such differences of opinion often give rise to disputes.

People often ask me, "Master, is there any difference between Buddhism and other religions?" I always reply that all true religions have the same goal: love. God and Jesus love all people equally. Buddhism emphasizes compassion, and all living beings are recipients of the Buddha's love. Therefore, true religions may have different names and scriptures, but they have one common end.

The true spirit of religion should be like that of the ocean, which accommodates the rivers and streams that flow to it. Thus, we must learn with a broad mind. To recognize only our own faith and excessively stress it over other religions is the wrong attitude to have.

We who are learning Buddhism must learn widely but also thoroughly so that we can fully understand not only ourselves but also others. We should know other people's dispositions as well as our own. When there is a conflict, we cannot simply say, "This is the way I am!" and expect other people to adapt to us. We must first try to understand other people's dispositions and try to be more accommodating. By so doing, disputes can be resolved peacefully.

I hope that whenever you are learning, you will open your mind to really understand yourself and also other people. Then you will be learning widely and thoroughly.

TO ELIMINATE ARROGANCE

The Buddha told us that it is very difficult to have a mind with both depth and forbearance, yet this is precisely what learning Buddhism is all about. Inside the Abode of Still Thoughts, I can hear pilgrims chanting the Buddha's name from afar and I can imagine their devotion and their humble postures. Their belief is like a pure stream that infuses and cleanses the anxious, restless mind. The purpose of spiritual cultivation is to fine-tune the mind and make it transparent and steadfast. In order to develop a mind that is broad and profound, we must first learn to get rid of all arrogance.

I mentioned in the previous chapter that it is difficult for us to study widely and thoroughly, because our minds are not broad enough. Even if our minds were broad enough, it would still be difficult to learn widely and thoroughly because our minds are changeable and unable to concentrate.

The Buddha also said, "It is difficult to eliminate arrogance." People tend to be proud and self-important and are rarely willing to humble themselves. In daily life, if we can treat people with a fair mind, we will be gentle in our manners. By so doing, society and every family in it will live in joy and peace.

PURE MINDS CREATE A PURE LAND

Looking at modern society, we see turbulence and insecurity. Why is this so? It is because people's minds are not calm. On television, we see political demonstrations in which someone in a mob shouts out slogans and others follow blindly, each person tougher and louder than the others. Scenes like this create a sense of instability.

Let us go back and listen to the chanting of the pilgrims outside the Abode. The sound is soft and soothing, like a pure stream purging us of our worries and cooling our feverish minds. And then observe how they move in unison. Compare this to the chaotic situations shown on TV. What a difference! Why do two groups of people in the same society display such different attitudes? Because the people who yell and fight harbor anger, jealousy and arrogance, while the pilgrims who have entered the world of Tzu Chi embrace compassionate love, forgiveness and open-mindedness.

Tzu Chi members are building a beautiful world for future generations, and at the same time they are purifying their own spirits and thoughts so as to create a perfect mind that is bright and pure. As a result, they look serene and peaceful. The sincerity that they demonstrate through chanting the Buddha's name and prostrating themselves before the Buddha's statue is an expression of truth, goodness and beauty. It is the best example of the Buddhist saying, "A pious mind is a Pure Land."

ARROGANCE IS A WEED THAT MUST BE REMOVED

A group of writers came to visit me once. They said to me, "It is very difficult to find someone in modern society who is comfortable with being ordinary. Since people now are more capable and ambitious, society has become chaotic because people aggressively promote their own interests."

One writer said to me, "A friend told me that he would be very happy if his daughter could find a husband who was physically and mentally healthy. He had no desire for her to find someone who was either very competent or successful."

"Having a healthy body is a blessing," I told them. "Having a fair and healthy mind means stability. Anyone who can lead a healthy, stable life is most fortunate."

Ordinary people tend to be egotistic, so the Buddha said that the twelfth difficulty is, "It is difficult to eliminate arrogance." It is even more difficult to study widely and thoroughly without becoming arrogant. The person who can achieve both is a real sage who can transcend mundane life. If arrogance is not eliminated, then no matter how capable one is, one will still be just an ordinary person.

Take a rice field for example. If it has rich soil but is not weeded, the crops will not grow properly. The farmer must first pull out all the weeds before applying fertilizer, lest the weeds outgrow the crops. Similarly, no matter how capable and learned a person is, if he is egotistic, his knowledge will be overshadowed by that negative attribute.

Learning to behave like the Buddha is to remove arrogance. Every morning during our morning prayer sessions, our minds are very pure, and we try to eliminate arrogance and distracting thoughts so that we can learn the Buddha's teachings with complete concentration. If we can maintain this state of mind in our daily lives and nurture a mentality of universal love and compassion, it will no longer be difficult to remove arrogance.

Therefore, we must remember to constantly examine ourselves in our daily lives. Have we acted from anger, jealousy or arrogance? Do we speak too loudly? Do we consider ourselves superior to others? If we have thought or acted in such ways, we must correct ourselves immediately. Then, like a patch of farmland that has been weeded and fertilized, our hearts will bear the abundant harvest of self-cultivation.

SELF-IMPORTANCE CAUSES SOCIAL UNREST

The current social situation in Taiwan is very unsettling. The cause is that there are too many self-important people. When two or more groups of people who are equally arrogant have differences of opinion, the conflict is usually resolved not through peaceful negotiation but clamorous demonstrations. The sounds of protest grow ever louder and society is filled with a violent atmosphere that makes people irritable and agitated. The result is physical confrontation, such as the fistfights in the legislature that we see on television. No wonder many people fear for the future of Taiwan.

The main cause for social unrest is the attitude of self-importance. What society needs now are common people, that is, people who do not view themselves as extraordinary. Such people would conduct themselves in a gentle manner. They would be polite and humble and respect others. In this way, society would become quiet and peaceful. What our society needs is for people to have ordinary minds. In the ordinary mind lies stability, freedom, joy and mutual respect. These are the things that will enhance the quality of our lives. The kind of life that we should pursue is one in which people respect one another. This is a life that is beautiful and peaceful.

However, arrogance is hard to uproot. It takes great effort for anyone to remove bad habits that have been with them for decades. This is why the Buddha said, "It is difficult to eliminate arrogance."

IT IS DIFFICULT
NOT TO LOOK DOWN ON
THOSE WHO KNOW LESS THAN YOU

H uman beings tend to be self-important and are consequently inclined to look down on other people. The Buddha once said, "It is difficult not to look down on someone who knows less than you," because ordinary people become rather arrogant when they become even a little famous.

Not Knowing Something Does Not Mean Not Being Able to Learn It

The Buddha taught us, "It is difficult not to look down on someone who knows less than you." Many people are not only egoistic, but treat others with contempt. Believing that they are more capable and knowledgeable than others, they are indignant over the fact that they have to do petty work. What's more, this kind of attitude has deep roots, so when they notice that someone is less capable than they are, they naturally begin to despise them. It is indeed quite difficult for those who consider themselves knowledgeable not to despise those who know less. Actually, no one in this world is born with any erudition, which must be accumulated over time and nurtured by a conducive environment. When someone knows less now, it does not mean that they will never learn, but simply that they have not started learning yet. Therefore, we must respect the people we meet and not look down on those who know less than we do.

The Buddha told us that there are four things we should not treat with disrespect. First, a spark of fire should not be ignored, since it can develop into a conflagration that sweeps a prairie. Second, a prince may be young, but he must not be treated with disrespect. When he comes of age, he will ascend the throne and govern his people. Therefore, a young prince must not be slighted. Third, a young dragon might be small, but it must not be treated with disrespect. Ancient Chinese believed that the four seasons came and went regularly because the dragon king in the sea was in control. Sun and rain were determined by the dragon king. Human beings needed their crops to stay alive, and harvests depended on the right weather. Thus, people in the past always felt great fear and respect towards the dragon king. The young dragon might be small, but someday it would have the wind and rain at its command. Fourth, a young Buddhist monk must not be slighted. The young monk will grow older and in the process gradually learn the dharma and expand his knowledge of Buddhism. His growing wisdom will allow him to become a teacher of Buddhism some day. So the young monk must not be looked down on.

We can see that what the Buddha wanted us to do was to always have a respectful attitude towards others. There are many little people and events in the world, but we must not despise any of them.

THE EMPEROR AND THE COWHERD

In ancient China, Huang-Ti [the "Yellow Emperor," reigned 2697–2597 BC] went to visit someone named Ta Kui, who lived on Chu Tsu Mountain. However, he and six companions got lost on the way. Just as they were at a loss for directions, they ran into a boy herding his cows. Huang-Ti approached him and asked, "Do you know the way to Chu Tsu Mountain?" The boy said he did and pointed out the direction for them.

Huang-Ti then asked him, "Do you know where Ta Kui lives?"

The boy replied, "Sure, I do."

Huang-Ti was surprised and said, "You are so young, but you seem to know quite a lot!" He then continued: "Do you know how to run a country?"

The boy said to him, "Yes I do. It is like herding cattle. Once you subdue the wild nature of the cattle, then they are tamed and easy to manage. Isn't a country governed the same way?"

Huang-Ti was very impressed and realized that this child could not be disregarded. Originally, he thought that the boy was young and ignorant. He did not expect that the philosophy the child had learned from his daily life could be applied to govern a country. We should take a lesson from this: we must not treat people and events lightly.

Subconsciously, everyone has a tendency to despise others. That is why the Buddha said, "It is difficult not to look down on some one who knows less than you." However, since we are learning Buddhism, we cannot consider this to be a difficulty. On the contrary, we must respect others and adjust ourselves accordingly. We should respect not only the elderly but also the young, because the younger generation will become the future pillars of the nation.

If everyone remembers to respect other people, others will react in the same manner. For as the old Chinese saying goes, "Anyone who respects others will be respected, and anyone who loves others will be loved."

IT IS DIFFICULT
TO HAVE AN OBJECTIVE MIND

I mentioned in the last chapter that it is difficult not to look down on those who know less than we do. We must treat all people with fairness and respect. It is very wrong if we are arrogant and constantly consider ourselves as being better and more capable than others. On the other hand, if we are unable to learn a certain task, we should not think, "It is your business that you are so competent and my business that I am not, so you should not look down on me and I need not look up to you." This is self-deceiving pride originating from feelings of inferiority, and it is also the wrong attitude to have.

BEING SMART DOES NOT MEAN BEING WISE

Those who study Buddhism must learn to be respectful to other people at all times. Even if we ourselves are very knowledgeable, we should not belittle those who are less so. A Chinese saying goes, "One may distinguish himself in any walk of life." It is not true that only people who have a lot of book-learning can make something of their lives. Knowing only the theories but not the practicalities is quite useless.

Some people do not know any profound philosophy or theory, but they know how to treat people right and do things the proper way. Someone who knows how to treat other people right and do the right things is a good person. A person who does no wrong and treats no one badly will have a good life.

In our society, there are many so-called "intelligent" criminals. They are able to use loopholes in the law to their advantage to commit shocking crimes. Being smart does not guarantee good deeds, so it is not something to brag about, nor is it a reason for holding less gifted people in contempt. On the other hand, people who are less competent should not feel inferior either. Self-deceiving pride, as much as arrogance, will cause people to shy away from or become indifferent to interpersonal relationships.

When we are learning Buddhism, we must first have a good perception of the ways and philosophies of this world. In this way, we will be able to form good relationships with others. If we simply know a lot of theories but cannot get along with other people, thus failing to achieve interpersonal harmony, then we will not reach true enlightenment. People with true wisdom should have broad minds that can embrace all people and events.

Having a broad mind means that you have a big heart, large enough to accommodate all kinds of people—you appreciate good people and tolerate the bad. A broad mind is like the sky that shelters all things beneath it and the earth that carries all things on top of it. Only with a broad mind can you avoid arrogance or self-deceiving pride.

IT IS DIFFICULT TO TREAT ALL PEOPLE EQUALLY

Aside from having a broad mind, we should also try to have an objective mind and treat all things equally. Indeed, as the Buddha told us, it is difficult for ordinary people to do so. But are we satisfied with being just ordinary? We are learning Buddhism precisely because we want to transcend the mundane. We must study the dharma to a level where our minds are like heaven and earth which ignore nothing, no matter how tiny it is, and the great earth which steadily carries all things, no matter how large they are. In sum, we should have broad minds and treat all people equally, whether they are rich or poor, intelligent or obtuse. This is the mind that treats all things equally.

Since the Buddha pointed out that it is difficult to have an impartial mind, he must have known that ordinary people have a deep-rooted habit of being partial. Many people talk about universal love, but it is not really easy for people to regard all things and events impartially. Everyone has someone they especially like and care about. It is very common. Even the great educator Confucius had a favorite disciple, Yen Yuan. How could a sage like Confucius prefer one disciple over the others? It was because when Yen Yuan heard one theory from Confucius, he could comprehend all related theories. Another disciple, Tzu Kung, once said, "When I hear one theory, I understand one; but when Yen Yuan hears one, he understands ten." Thus, even Confucius differentiated between his disciples based on their ability to understand his teachings. This is "discrimination."

GIVE OUR BLESSINGS TO PEOPLE WHO ARE AGAINST US

When even Confucius was unable to treat all people equally, what can be expected of ordinary people like ourselves? As a matter of fact, the Buddha himself felt closer to some of his disciples than to others. Ananda was very dear to the Buddha, because he took care of the Buddha's daily needs. On the other hand, the Buddha felt quite helpless towards another disciple, Devadatta.

Ananda, who acted as the Buddha's personal assistant, was concerned about everything the Buddha did, whereas Devadatta was always plotting against the Buddha. Of course, the Buddha tolerated him and harbored no hatred against him. In the *Wonderful Lotus Sutra*, we read that Devadatta eventually attained buddhahood, courtesy of the Buddha's tireless guidance. Although the Buddha was able to return virtue for hatred, he still often felt powerless towards Devadatta. Since even the Buddha faced this kind of dilemma, what about common people like ourselves?

Nonetheless, we must try to emulate his forgiveness and repay hatred with virtue. Remember, the Buddha gave his blessings to even the most reprehensible disciple. Therefore, we should also give our blessings silently to people who bear grudges against us and hope that in the future they will have great fortune and virtue. If we can do this, then we are treating all people equally.

The myriad things in this world could not possibly be on the same level. If everything in this world were equal, it would not be this world anymore. There are high mountains and deep oceans; things are large and small, tall and short. Even the verdant grasses and trees in a single garden are not equally tall. And just like all the other things in the world, our minds are sometimes high, sometimes low, sometimes tender and sometimes hard.

However, since we are learning Buddhism, we must do our best to remind ourselves of our goal and set our minds to harbor only love towards others. We may feel powerless towards some people, but we still have to treat them with an accommodating mind and bear no resentment. When we feel that we do not know how to deal with others, it actually means that we still have the heart to guide and help them. But if we resent them, we will create an even worse relationship with them in this life and for many lives to come. Endless bad karma will thus be accumulated.

NURTURE AN UNBIASED MIND

In spring the weather changes quickly. Yesterday the sun was out and a breeze was blowing; today it is rainy and windy. The natural world changes drastically, and so do our minds. The Buddha advised us to have minds that are as tranquil as water. However, even water can have waves!

It is very difficult for anyone to keep a level mind when facing the outside world. For instance, yesterday's weather and today's weather are obviously not the same, so it is impossible to say that we don't feel any difference. Outside, cocks crow and birds chirp; it would be difficult to say that we don't hear anything and that it is quiet. When there is any change in the external world, our minds naturally change with it. Nature brings us cold, heat, wind and rain, and our bodies and minds change accordingly. But then what of the Buddha's admonition to us that we should not have discriminatory minds?

First let us examine what it means not to have a discriminatory mind. Many people are keen on spiritual cultivation. Some like to go to temples, and some believe that meditation or chanting sutras is the means of reaching transcendence. These people go so far as to think that their methods of cultivation are the best and their sect is the only promulgator of the authentic Buddhist teachings. As for the Tzu Chi commissioners who tirelessly raise funds and help the needy, they are often criticized for not studying Buddhist teachings, thus cultivating only blessings and not wisdom. This is a discriminatory remark. The commissioners may refute it by saying, "Helping the poor is cultivating blessings, and educating the rich to give to the poor is cultivating wisdom! You people only care about yourselves—this is having wisdom but no blessings. What is the use of that?" Yet they would also be speaking in a discriminatory manner.

We must understand that in Buddhism there are eighty-four thousand ways to carry out spiritual cultivation. This is because there are all kinds of people in the world and they need different methods of self-cultivation. People who are cultivating themselves must adapt to their environment but not be changed by it. We were lucky enough to be born in the world as human beings, to learn the Buddha's teachings and to do good for others, so we must cherish our good fortune. We and other people with similar goals of helping people should cherish the chance to work together for the well-being of the human race and to complete the mission of the bodhisattvas. If we do not have the opportunity to work with others or do not share the same commitment, we must not argue with them or push them into doing anything. This is having a mind that is not discriminatory.

RICH AND POOR, GIVER AND RECEIVER, ALL ARE THE SAME

When the Buddha was alive, he constantly encouraged his disciples to both give and receive alms equitably. At that time, there was a large gap between the rich and the poor in India. It is still the same now. If you go to India, you will see many homeless wanderers dressed in rags. On the other end of the social scale, rich people decorate their mansions with gold, silver and jade. From ancient to present times, the situation in India has remained largely the same.

When the Buddha and the monks received meals from kings or ministers, they accepted them as they would from anyone else. After the meal was finished, the Buddha would speak to the almsgivers with joy and gratitude, wanting and giving nothing else. There were also extremely poor people. One poor old woman was completely destitute, but she still wanted to give something to the Buddha. She saw that many people brightened the Buddha's lecture hall with oil lamps, so she cut off her hair in exchange for an oil lamp. The Buddha accepted it with great gratitude and admiration. Thus, the person who receives always feels the same gratitude towards the giver, regardless of the material value of the goods. This is the unbiased mind of the receiver.

The rich gave the Buddha garments made of gold, while the poor old woman cut off her hair in order to give the Buddha an oil lamp. In both cases, the donors were giving the best they had with the utmost sincerity. This is the unbiased mind of the giver.

GIVING TO THE POOR IS AS MERITORIOUS AS GIVING TO THE BUDDHA

Long, long ago, after the Maitreya Bodhisattva gave a meal to the Nansheng Buddha, he also gave some food to a beggar and gave the remainder to a dog. When the Nansheng Buddha saw this, he joyfully praised the Maitreya Bodhisattva and said, "You achieve the same merits for giving to a buddha, a beggar and a dog." When Maitreya gave alms to the buddha, it was with respect and devotion. When he gave to the beggar, it was with compassion and love. When he fed the dog, he did it simply to relieve its hunger, seeking nothing in return. That was why the Nan-sheng Buddha said that the merit obtained for giving to a dog was the same as the merit obtained for giving to a buddha.

Most people would say, "I receive more merits from offering to an enlightened monk or nun!" Actually, it depends on the almsgivers' state of mind when they give. The rarest kind of merit comes from almsgiving without regard for the cost and without expecting to receive anything in return. Although giving to a buddha brings great merit, if the giver has the intention of receiving merit, then the giver is not giving with an unbiased heart.

I remember many years ago when Master Tao Yuan was still alive, someone asked him, "I hear that Tzu Chi members cultivate only blessings but not wisdom—what is your view on that?"

The Master replied, "The merit obtained from giving to the poor is the same as the merit obtained from giving to Buddhist monks or nuns. In fact, giving to the poor is even more meritorious than giving to the masters, and the giver cultivates both blessings and wisdom!"

The person who asked the question thought this was a strange remark, so he asked Master Tao Yuan to explain it to him. "When you give to a Buddhist master, deep inside your heart you are hoping for something in return, but when you give to a poor person or a beggar, you do not seek anything," Master Tao Yuan explained. "It is because of the sincere, unbiased compassion and love and the wisdom that originates from them that the merit obtained is so great."

From this example, we understand what is meant by having an objective mind. People usually make distinctions between rich and poor, giver and receiver; but if we give what we can, ask for nothing in return and keep ourselves unbiased, then we have the correct attitude to conduct spiritual cultivation and also to treat all people equitably.

IT IS DIFFICULT
NOT TO CRITICIZE OTHERS

The atmosphere of the early morning makes us fresh and spirited, and the chirping of the birds gives us a keener sense of the quietude of the land. But then the sound of a train roaring by disrupts the natural tranquillity. There are many sounds in our daily lives. There are the beautiful sounds of nature that belong to gentle breezes, drizzling rain, chirping birds and busy insects. Then there are artificial sounds, such as the noise of machinery in action and of people talking.

PERSONAL CULTIVATION IS EVIDENT FROM ONE'S WORD AND CONDUCT

There are two ways of expressing ourselves in daily life: sound and appearance. Sound refers to language and speech; appearance refers to manner of conduct. If you speak and act in a way that is agreeable to other people, this suggests that you are well cultivated. On the other hand, if your words and actions offend people, then you need more refinement.

In conversing with others, we must control the volume of our voices. Based on the distance between ourselves and our listeners, we adjust our voices to a volume that is just loud enough for the other party to hear us clearly. If our voices are so low that they cannot hear us, we are being disrespectful. If they are close to us but we still speak too loudly, it is both rude and annoying to our listeners. These are signs of an uncultivated person. Just imagine, if there are so many things we need to pay attention to regarding the volume of our voice, then how many other things must we take into consideration regarding our other conduct!

People tend to treat other people in accordance with their likes and dislikes. If we feel friendly towards someone, we speak highly of their good side and cover up their shortcomings. When we dislike someone, we do not mention anything about them that is praiseworthy. Instead, we find the tiniest fault and grab the chance to slander them. This is the evil karma created by the mouth—the words we speak that expose our fondness or distaste for other people. The mouth is the gate through which our inner thoughts are expressed. But most of us open our mouths and move our tongues to make biased remarks about other people, so we must be very careful.

TRUTH CANNOT BE FULLY CONVEYED THROUGH LANGUAGE

The Buddha said that it was difficult not to criticize others. This is indeed so, because ordinary people make favorable or unfavorable comments on other people or events all the time. The Buddha also said, "Truth is not to be described in words," because genuine philosophy or truth cannot be comprehensively defined by words. Come to think of it, are the ideas that I am telling you correct or not? If we consider the phrase, "Truth is not described in words," then what I have told you is not the ultimate truth!

But then again, there are still many things that need to be conveyed through language. If there is no verbal communication, how will we express our own feelings? The goal of spiritual cultivation is to be able to generate calmness and harmony with our speech. When we have reached this level, then we are really learning the dharma.

There is a short story in *Chuang Tzu*. A person named Tai Ching once visited an enlightened person named Wu Chiung [literally "without end"]. Tai Ching said, "I heard that you have profound knowledge of everything from heaven to earth. Therefore I wonder if you can tell me what is the Great Way of the universe." Wu Chiung's reply was short, "I cannot."

Tai had traveled a long distance to visit Wu Chiung and was naturally disappointed at this answer. Some time later, a person named Wu Wei [literally "without action"] was recommended to him. He put the same question to Wu Wei, who was able to give him an answer, "The Great Way of the universe is something that can be either invaluable or without value, of infinite size or infinitesimal size." However, Tai was still not quite satisfied with this answer.

Tai then went to visit a person named Wu Shih [literally "without beginning"], to whom he related his search for the Great Way of the universe. "Wu Chiung told me that he doesn't know the answer, but Wu Wei said he does. Which one of them is right?" "Between knowing and not knowing," Wu Shih replied, "the one who knows only understands the basics, the one who does not know is the one that has grasped the profound meaning of the Great Way. Because the real Way cannot be described in words. What can be put into words is only a very limited part of the truth of the universe. The whole truth is simply impossible to be conveyed through language."

From this story we see that people who understand the truth will not seek to display their understanding through language. They know that words are not an adequate medium of expression. Since the truth cannot be fully and clearly expressed through daily speech, they might as well not talk about it at all.

TREATING OTHERS EQUALLY AND WITHOUT PREJUDICE

When we communicate with other people, we must be very careful and notice whether we are remaining impartial. If we are prejudiced, then what is good may be described as bad and vice versa. Biased criticism will mislead people into forming wrong judgments of the person in question. Therefore, we must regard others with a fair mind and refrain from commenting on others based on our personal feelings towards them.

In addition, we must not say that we know something when in fact we don't, for that would be overestimating our own wisdom and thus exposing ourselves to ridicule. Therefore, in our daily lives, we have to be mindful of what we say. We must not think that speaking is easy, nor should we think that since we are not verbally abusing others, it doesn't matter if we just gossip a little. It does matter! Because our cultivation and decency is within the words we utter.

The Buddha said that it was difficult not to criticize others, but we must transform this difficulty into something that is achievable. And how should we do this? Just as I mentioned earlier: sometimes we simply do not know whether we should say something or not, so what should we do? We have to be mindful.

IT IS DIFFICULT
TO FIND A GOOD FRIEND
WHO CAN HELP AND INSPIRE YOU

As students of Buddhism, if we can cast away our prejudices, we will find that everything in the universe carries some form of the dharma, the Buddhist message. The Buddha said, "Truth is not to be described in words." So we should try to find the truth that the Buddha wanted to impart to us with a simple mind and genuine sincerity.

The Buddha said, "It is difficult to find a good friend who can help and inspire you." It is difficult enough to distance yourself from gossips and bad friends, and even more so to meet a friend who can really help and inspire you. And what is to be expected of such a friend? It is someone who can inspire your conscience and wisdom; it is someone who guides you and helps you solve your problems; it is someone who transports you from the dark land of the ordinary person to the bright realm of the sage. Yet in reality, how many people like this—people who help you smooth out your worries, round off your sharp edges and remove your biases—can be found?

Finding someone who can guide and inspire you is indeed difficult. Suppose you find this person but are unable to cast away your biases, then even if the most inspiring person in the world were standing in front of you, you still would not be able to benefit from their knowledge and instruction. This is why there is a saying: "When perception is clouded by prejudice, an inspiring and helpful friend is impossible to come across."

GOOD WORDS MAY CARRY BAD INTENTIONS

If each one of us can remove our biases, then the words of good people will help us solve our worries. Spiritual cultivation helps us maintain our original nature. If we have delusive thoughts, we will not be able to see the truth and our passions will be confused. Words uttered with the best intentions might be mistaken for mean comments if the listener judges those words with a biased mind, thus completely distorting the original goodwill of the speaker.

We do this all the time: suspecting other people of being prejudiced against us when they are really only pointing out the truth. When we see other people talking among themselves, we often assume that they are making disparaging or libelous remarks about us. This is self-incurred agitation, caused by foolish delusions. If we cannot eliminate our delusive assumptions, then we will be too blind to understand and accept even the most wonderful Buddhist ideas. Therefore, we must face the world with our unadulterated nature. If we can do this, then even the songs of birds and crows of cocks will carry the teachings of Buddhism, because these are the sounds that inspire our innate selves with spontaneity and purity.

In Japan, there is a short story in an elementary school textbook, used to foster the pure, simple minds of children. This is how the story goes:

A hunter aimed his gun at a bird sitting in a tree. Suddenly, just as the hunter was about to fire, ants bit him. The hunter's hand moved slightly and he missed the bird. So the bird was saved. How did this come to happen? The bird once saw a group of ants struggling in the water, so it picked up a leaf with its beak, dropped it into the water, and saved all the ants from drowning. So, when the hunter was about to shoot the bird, the ants came to its rescue.

The Japanese use this story to demonstrate the cause and effect concept of "You plant such a cause and receive such a result."

ANY LIVING BEING CAN BE SOMEONE'S TEACHER

There is a similar story in China. During the Chin dynasty (265–420 AD), there was a twelve-year-old child of a poor family, his name was Mao Pao. Mao's family lived in northern China, where temperatures drop very low during winter and it often snows. One day, Mao went to watch fishermen work by the river. When one of the fishermen pulled in his net, there were some fish and an adorable small white turtle in it. The fisherman picked up the turtle and said happily, "Wonderful! White turtles are very rare, and this one is so white that it shines! It is definitely worth a fortune!"

Someone wanted to cook the white turtle and eat it, and someone else wanted to put it on display to make money. Mao felt sorry for the turtle and asked the fisherman to set it free. But the fisherman felt that it was a rare chance to catch such a precious turtle, so he simply did not want to let it go. The child looked at the turtle and the turtle also looked up at the child with expressive eyes, as though it were pleading for its life. Great pity filled the child's heart. He took off his coat and held it over his head with both hands, then he knelt down on both legs. With the utmost sincerity, he asked the fisherman to let the turtle go and said that he was willing to exchange his coat for its freedom.

The fisherman was moved by the boy's compassion, especially since Mao was willing to sacrifice the only heavy clothing he had in the midst of the bitter cold weather. However, the fisherman was not so moved as to be willing to give the turtle to the child for nothing, so he took the coat from the child. The fisherman said, "This white turtle is worth much more than the coat, but I'm impressed by your sincerity, so I will swap with you."

Mao joyfully embraced the little white turtle. "You are safe," he said. "Although I'm suffering from the piercingly cold wind, I saved your life. This was definitely worth it!" The turtle seemed to understand the boy's words. It shed tears of gratitude and nodded its head at the child. The child then gently carried the turtle to the riverbank and set it free.

Twenty years later, Mao became a general and led his army to many victories. One time he led tens of thousands of troops into a battle, but their enemy was very strong and surrounded them. Mao and his remaining soldiers were able to break through the enemy's blockade and run to the Yangtze River. Behind them were enemy troops, before them the great river. He ordered the soldiers to take any boat that was available. When all the soldiers had safely left, he looked around and found not even a skiff in sight and his enemies drawing near. Without much thought, he jumped into the river.

The water was flowing rapidly and he had to struggle hard against the flow for his life. Just as he passed out from exhaustion, something emerged from the river and raised him above the water. When he came to, he saw a blanket of white snow around him and found that he was lying on the back of a big white turtle. He recognized the turtle as the same one that he rescued twenty years ago. And, just as it had done twenty years ago, the turtle looked at Mao with tears of gratitude in its eyes. It was truly incredible!

When Mao had reached the shore, the white turtle departed reluctantly for the river. As it swam forward, it kept looking back at him and nodding at him. The turtle seemed happy that it had finally repaid the favor it had received from the general twenty years before.

The general was very grateful, and he wondered at the close relationship that could be formed between human beings and animals. He wondered why human beings invaded each other's territories and killed one another. If there could be so much regard between animals and human beings, why was it that people could not love and respect each other? Disillusioned by worldly life, he resigned from the army, went into seclusion and practiced spiritual cultivation.

The Buddha told us that it is difficult to meet someone who can help and inspire us. Why is it hard? Because people criticize others and treat them unfairly. Once they have preconceptions, they act with discrimination towards people. If they like a person, they want to have this person all to themselves and become angry and jealous if someone else is friendly with that person. This kind of discrimination comes from biased affection.

Some people have many prejudices, but they never reflect on their inner world. If someone tries to point out their mistakes and give them helpful advice, they think that person is being sarcastic. When people base their judgment of people and events on such prejudices, how will they ever meet anyone who will be able to inspire them?

The two stories we just read look at the world through childlike ingenuousness, which is why all the creatures described were able to coexist in harmony. However, many people have views that are distorted by delusions and tainted by prejudices. For them, friction with other people is unavoidable.

When we carry out spiritual cultivation, we must return to our pure, genuine nature. We should subdue our egos, open our hearts to all people, and protect and assist others. If we can do so, a sentence spoken by a child can teach and inspire us, and even the behavior of a mentally disturbed person can be an admonition to us. Then, the forms and sounds of everything in the universe can teach and inspire us and lead us to see the truth. As long as we use our observation and see the natural world and all people with a direct and simple mind, we will understand the truth that is contained in them.

EVEN CONFUCIUS WOULD ASK HUMBLY

There is a Chinese saying, "Even if you have acquaintances all over the world, how many of them are your true friends?" This describes how hard it is to find a good friend or a mentor. The same message is conveyed by what the Buddha said: it is difficult to meet someone who can help and inspire us. It means that it is quite impossible for every person you meet to become your good friend or teacher.

Having been born into this world, we all have a lot to learn, so much that a lifetime of diligent study is not enough. Confucius was an unassuming person and a diligent student. He considered anyone who could enlighten him, even a child, to be his teacher. For sages and saints, there is no end to the pursuit of knowledge.

Confucius said, "When three men walk together, one of them must be my teacher; I will choose to follow what is good and correct what is not good." When I am in the company of two other persons, there must be someone who I can learn from, who can be my model, while there must be someone whose mistakes will also teach me a lesson. When we see what is not good in a person, we will reflect on our own actions and warn ourselves not to be like him. We see in him actions that are offensive and temperament that is disagreeable. This person actually deserves our gratitude because they are living examples of what we should not be. On the other hand, we should emulate the virtuous person because he represents the bright side of life. He has a positive attitude that brings joy to other people and admiration unto himself. And this is the person that we should learn from.

However, ordinary people have closed minds and think that they are capable of doing everything. Even if they have faults, they console themselves by thinking, "My faults are my business. Why should I worry whether other people have any good points that I should be learning from?" This is the logic of the ordinary mind. To correct this wrong mindset, we should be in touch with our desire to learn and study with diligence from day to day.

Mutual Help and Encouragement between Tzu Chi Members

Looking back on the time when Tzu Chi was first established, there were only thirty commissioners, but they shared the same views and were willing to reduce their personal expenses to realize the mission of great love. Because they were all of one mind, they saw each other as their model, encouraged each other and devoted much time and effort to the establishment of Tzu Chi, which owes everything to them. Now, more than three decades later, the number of commissioners has grown tremendously.

The Tzu Chi commissioners are examples of helpful and inspiring people. One person influences another person, and then another, ever expanding the circle of compassionate people who have been inspired to practice charitable deeds. After they begin learning about Buddhism and Tzu Chi, they change their own views of life and influence the people around them. Their transformation leads them to interact harmoniously with other people, proving that they made the right choice and that it has had a positive effect on them. This in turn inspires family and friends to follow their example. The chain of mutually inspiring and encouraging people then becomes longer and longer. Right now, millions of people around the world have become part of this great chain, giving help and inspiration to yet more people around them.

One commissioner told me that an overseas Chinese from the Netherlands came back to Taiwan several months ago because he wanted to learn more about the Tzu Chi spirit. This commissioner took the visitor to our offices in Taichung and Taipei. After witnessing all the activities organized by Tzu Chi, he was truly moved by our spirit. He vowed to become a member of Tzu Chi and to begin promoting the spirit of Tzu Chi as soon as he returned to the Netherlands. And so he did. Not long after he left Taiwan, this overseas Chinese recruited more than twenty people to become members of Tzu Chi.

I would like to emphasize not how many members we have in the Netherlands, but the fact that an inspired Tzu Chi member crossed the ocean to a foreign land, carried out the missions of Tzu Chi and spread the spirit of Buddhism. Currently, Tzu Chi members in many Western countries have already begun to propagate Chinese culture and the Buddhist spirit of "great mercy even to strangers and great compassion to all."

Helpful and inspirational people are difficult to find, but in the world of Tzu Chi they are everywhere. I often see processions of pilgrims that stretch all the way from the main road to the Abode of Still Thoughts. I look from the Abode at the long, winding line of people prostrating themselves with great piety, and I wonder how many people must be moved by this scene, by these pilgrims whose actions are so inspirational.

Sometimes it rains and there is mud on the ground, but still the pilgrims keep on walking towards the Abode, prostrating themselves at every third step. The scene is very touching and demonstrates the beauty of the Tzu Chi world. We can encourage and push each other forward, so every person is helpful and inspirational to us. This is why I say, contrary to what the Buddha told us, that it is not hard to find a helpful friend in Tzu Chi.

And the same could be said of people who are not in Tzu Chi. Because as long as we harbor a mind that wants to learn and meet people who can teach us, then everyone is an example for us to learn from. Some people lament that they may have acquaintances all over the world, but not many close friends. But in fact, every single person in the world can be our close friend and teacher—if we want them to.

There are many wonderful stories of charity in Tzu Chi. What may be hard for most people to do is not so hard for Tzu Chi members, who make their lives most meaningful and valuable. I once said that a buddha's mind is a mind of great compassion, and a bodhisattva's mind is a mind of joyful giving. Since we are followers of the Buddha, we must nurture compassionate minds. In order to reach the level of the Buddha, we must first practice the Path of the Bodhisattvas; and to practice the Path of the Bodhisattvas, we must give joyfully. We must give not only material goods, but also our own strength, even if it means giving up our lives for the sake of all living beings. After we have devoted our time and money and given up our insignificant personal love for great universal love, only then can we say that we are truly practicing joyful giving. If everyone in the world has compassion and is able to give joyfully, then everyone will be that someone who can help and inspire us, and everyone will be our teacher and good friend.

IT IS DIFFICULT
TO FIND YOUR TRUE NATURE AND
LEARN THE WAY OF ENLIGHTENMENT

T he Buddha said, "It is difficult to find your true nature and learn the way of enlightenment." People who are able to behold their true selves and become enlightened are very rare.

Most people first start out to practice spiritual cultivation with great confidence and pursue Buddhist teachings with enthusiasm. However, all people are inclined to be negligent or ignorant. Negligent means that we become lazy and cannot sustain the enthusiasm we had in the beginning. If we could maintain the first motivation that prompted us to begin our spiritual cultivation and the determination to seek the Buddha's teachings and to sacrifice our life to acquire the truth, it would become easy to obtain a thorough understanding of Buddhism. However, this is difficult for the ordinary person to do.

Then there is the weakness of ignorance. All living beings have the same pure, good, innocent nature, which is also the wisdom that we are all born with. But we tend to look past it and seek goodness and wisdom outside ourselves. In this way, we lose sight of our own nature and waste our time leading an ignorant life.

THE BUDDHA-NATURE IS WITHIN, NOT WITHOUT

During the Warring States period (475–222 BC) in ancient China, warlords seized different parts of China. In the state of Yen, there was a child who heard that people in the state of Chao walked gracefully because drama was thriving there and there were many performers of the art. The boy wanted very much to learn their elegant style of walking, so he went to Chao and stayed there for several years. As it turned out, the boy not only failed to acquire the new style of walking, but forgot how he originally walked. In the end, the boy had to crawl all the way back to Yen.

Although this is an improbable story, many people are in fact just like that boy from the state of Yen: they have lost touch with what they always had—their innate buddha-nature. Any healthy child will learn to walk within a certain time after birth because it is a human instinct to walk. That boy from Yen wanted to abandon his own natural way of walking and learn the artificial style used in drama performances. In the end he failed to learn anything new, and at the same time he lost his original ability to walk normally. Buddhists want to find their pure buddha-nature, but how come it never occurs to them to look inside themselves?

One day, the Tzu Chi Junior College of Nursing held a carnival. The students and their families gathered on the playground and played a game in which each team had to come up with whatever object the moderator named, and the team that produced the most of that certain object was the winner. Everyone, including the college president and her husband, participated in the game. The students were completely spontaneous. When they needed something, they would ask for it from whoever was in sight, whether they knew them or not. Everyone joined in the merrymaking. If some strands of hair were needed, students would simply stick out their heads and let their teammates take their pick. They also borrowed shoelaces or belts from anyone who happened to be there. In the end, even the president's shoes were borrowed!

Then they ran a three-legged race. People of all ages and all ranks were mingled and grouped together. When they fell, they got up again and kept on running. No one really cared who won the game. The only important thing was that everyone thoroughly enjoyed themselves. And that, after all, was the purpose of playing the game.

Life ought to be the same. We should cherish our innate nature and stop thinking of our own interests. Understand that as long as we have fulfilled our responsibilities, it does not matter anymore whether we win or lose. In our lives, it is very important that we don't lose touch with our true nature, which is the same for people of all ages. When we are learning Buddhism, the first thing we must do is to return to our original selves and comprehend our nature.

SEIZE THE GOOD THOUGHT OF THIS MOMENT

We often lose the good thought we have at a certain moment. For example, we say we are going to do something generous, but regret it the next minute. Perhaps we feel bad one day for some mistake we made the day before. People often regret past actions or events. It is because we do not have firm control of our thoughts and do not understand ourselves completely. This is why I often say, "We must guard the thought of the present moment."

When people ask me what plans I have for my life, I always reply, "I have a great goal that I want to realize by

177

holding on to every second of the here and now." Because if I can guard my present thought, I will not do or say the wrong things or become negligent or confused.

We ought to earnestly guard over every thought of every moment in our lives. However, we tend to lose track of our thoughts and live our days in confusion. We are careless in dealing with people and events, and then we regret it afterwards. When we should let bygones be bygones, we start feeling sorry for what we did and waste our present thoughts on futile worries.

The Buddha said that it was difficult to find our nature and learn the way of enlightenment because people often lose the thought that belongs to the here and now. In sum, it is because we cannot guard over our present thoughts that what is easy becomes difficult. If we have firm control of our thoughts and know our true nature through and through, then learning the way of enlightenment becomes a simple thing.

COMPREHEND THE BUDDHA'S MIND

Each living being has its own function and nature. Listen to the sounds of the earth in the early morning.

Cocks crow to herald the morning. Birds sing and flowers emit their fragrances. These living beings are all carrying out their functions according to their natures.

As a matter of fact, we human beings also have our original functions and nature. Buddhist monks and nuns living in temples rise before dawn. Whether they recite sutras or prostrate themselves in front of the Buddha's statue, they all have one thought—to pursue Buddhism. They reduce their sleeping time and rise at three or four in the morning out of the desire to enhance their understanding of Buddhism and to seek the truth.

But even though we want to, will we really be able to behold the true nature of the Buddha? Can we really return to our innate nature or even attain enlightenment? When we chant the Buddha's name, do we really comprehend the buddha-nature? Putting these questions aside, let us first reflect upon our daily behavior and speech. How many bad habits do we have? And how many have we been able to detect and eliminate? Most of us do not even understand ourselves, so how are we to understand the nature of the Buddha?

We often say, "There is no difference between the mind, the Buddha and all living beings." This is easy to say, but actually we do not fully comprehend the purport of this simple concept. Most of us know the nature of equality, innocence and freedom only as defined by words. People rarely realize that the mind of the true self is very close to the mind of the Buddha. This is why the Buddha seems so distant. Many people have the form of human beings but are unable to carry out the functions belonging to one, so their human forms are useless. If they can use the functions of their human bodies to do good, their minds will become close to the Buddha's mind. But most ordinary people can never do this. That is why they are merely living beings who are very distant from the Buddha.

Chickens crow and dogs bark, but they are incapable of understanding the existence of truth. This is because animals do not have intellectual power. An animal may have a nature that is innocent and pure, but it does not have any chance of being enlightened and discovering the truth. Thus, they are on a level that is extremely far from the level of the Buddha. Human beings have intellectual perception. The environment around us provides situations from which we experience and learn and which spur us to reflect upon ourselves. Therefore, we have the best opportunity to be able to get close to the buddha-nature.

But unfortunately, many people simply let their chances slip away and give up the opportunity to perceive their genuine nature. Instead they study unreal mysticism and seek supernatural powers. This is not the intent or goal of learning Buddhism.

DO NOT REGRET THE THOUGHT OF THE PAST MOMENT

As Buddhists, what we really seek is to be in control of our thought of this moment and not to regret now the thought of the past moment. Only in this way will we have a steady mind to pursue Buddhism. If we are always regretting our past mistakes, dwelling on the wrong things that we said or did, then we will not be able to concentrate on the people and events of this moment. If we seek to understand the thoughts of others without first being able to steady our own thoughts, we will easily deviate from the path of the Buddha and tread the path of evil.

The correct attitude to have in learning Buddhism is to face the reality of our present lives. We must examine how much potential we have, and whether we have realized it to help others.

I once told a short story, as follows:

Before an old temple, there was a pond where many toads lived. The toads sometimes hopped into the pond and stayed there or hopped out of the pond to look at the world. Many practitioners of Buddhism came to the temple to burn incense and recite Buddhist sutras. Sometimes they walked in the square and chanted the Buddha's name while keeping count with their beads. When the toads jumped out of the pond and saw these practitioners walking so gracefully, they wished they could do the same.

One of the toads hopped to the entrance of the main sanctuary while the people were prostrating themselves before the statues. It prayed sincerely for the Buddha to grant him the ability to stand up on two feet and walk like humans.

A deity was moved by the toad's sincerity and granted its wish. The toad was overjoyed, because all the other toads had to jump with their four legs while it was the only one that could walk on two legs. It felt happy and proud.

One day, suddenly there came a snake. Most of the toads dove into the pond to hide from the snake. The toad that walked on two legs was also very frightened, but walking on two legs was after all not as fast as jumping with four legs, an ability it now lacked. In the end, the snake caught up with the toad. As it struggled in pain in the snake's mouth, the toad thought with deep regret, "Why did I give up my ability to jump? In order to walk on two legs, I end up getting eaten by a snake. But it's too late for regrets!"

Although this is just a children's story, it actually serves as a good warning for us. When we learn Buddhism, we recover our original nature and abilities. If we attempt to seek something that is beyond our reach, we will ultimately fail. Some people say they want to learn the way to enlightenment, but instead they become lost in the pursuit of supernatural powers and enter the realm of evil. Not only do their minds become confused, but they also lose forever their chances to pursue wisdom. This is truly a pity.

The original intent of learning Buddhism should be to apply the Buddha's teachings to our daily lives, to use them as sweet dew that cleanses away our ignorance and purges our tainted minds. The original goal of learning Buddhism is to cultivate the life functions that we neglected, and also to realize our capacity for pure love. We would be under the wrong impression if we think learning Buddhism is only about seeking supernatural powers.

It is my wish that all of us can comprehend our own nature and functions. If we fail to do so, even if we practice spiritual cultivation, it will be very difficult to obtain the truth. Actually, what is closest to us is our pure, genuine nature, but we ignore it and search for what is outside of us. Your eyes can see others clearly, but cannot see your own face. What is closest to us is actually overlooked or cannot be seen.

In learning Buddhism we should start from what is closest to us, and the simplest way is to make use of our inborn abilities to help the needy. Remember, we must not neglect what is close to us and seek something that is far away.

IT IS DIFFICULT
TO ENLIGHTEN PEOPLE
AT THE RIGHT OCCASIONS

T he sound of people solemnly chanting the Buddha's name can be heard a distance away from the Abode of Still Thoughts. Although I am meditating, I feel as if I am among the pilgrims and chanting along with them. Such an atmosphere makes one feel peaceful and joyful.

The eighteenth difficulty is, "It is difficult to enlighten people at the right occasions." To enlighten people is truly a difficult task. It is especially hard for people to like you at first sight and to be inspired by your conduct, speech and demeanor to reform themselves. But just as the pious pilgrims were able to make me feel tranquil and happy, with sincerity we will be able to move people.

UTMOST SINCERITY CAN TRANSFORM PEOPLE

I remember some years back, there was a row of pigsties next to the road that lead to the Abode. Next to the pigsties there was a huge fishpond. The owner dumped the pig manure into the pond to feed the fish. When the south wind blew in the summer, the stench from the pigsties would travel to the Abode. But the land did not belong to us, and if the landowner wanted to raise pigs and keep fish, there was nothing we could do.

One day, a group of around twenty Tzu Chi members made a pilgrimage to the Abode. At midnight they started to walk from the Suhua Highway, prostrating themselves every three steps. The landowner saw this and wondered what these people were up to. He could not understand why they kept kneeling down instead of walking normally. Back then, pilgrims prostrated themselves while chanting the Buddha's name silently. For a person who had no belief and who had never seen a pilgrimage before, it was natural to be curious and wary.

Nevertheless, the landowner went home and found a flashlight. He followed the pilgrims and brightened the road for them from behind. He did so because he had noticed that young people were tearing by on their motorcycles, and since it was dark and the pilgrims were dressed in black, he was worried that there might be an accident. So he held the flashlight to alert people on motorcycles or in cars that there were people on the road ahead of them. In this manner, he followed the pilgrims all the way to the Abode of Still Thoughts.

It was dawn already and he started to leave for home. At that moment, I walked out and saw him, so I greeted him. He said to me, "These people are very sincere!"

I told him, "This is called a 'pilgrimage.'"

"I've never seen anything like this before," he said. "It's really impressive."

After a moment, he sniffed the air. "Why does it smell like pig manure here?"

"It comes from your pigsties."

"I thought it only stank at my place. I didn't realize that the stench was even worse here."

"Do you think a situation like this is good?"

"No, no, certainly not. I tell you what: I'll stop raising pigs after I finish raising this batch." Later, he kept his word and closed the sties.

This is how people are moved by sincerity. Originally, the landowner kept hundreds of pigs. We could often hear the pigs whining as we were holding our morning prayers. It was always heartbreaking to hear the cries of the pigs just before they were sent to the slaughterhouse. Happily, the pilgrims moved the owner through their pious, sincere conduct.

After being in a pleasant environment for a long time, people start to appreciate it less. A saying best describes this: "After spending a long time in a room filled with orchids, people will not smell the fragrance anymore." To the same effect, "After spending a long time in a fish market, people will not smell its stench." When people have lived in a filthy environment for too long, they lose their sensitivity to bad smells.

Mind Alone Creates Heaven and Hell

A few years after the Buddha attained enlightenment, his father invited him to return to his homeland to lecture on Buddhism. On the second day of his return, the Buddha went out at noon to ask for alms. As he passed the royal palace, he saw a couple that were obviously very much in love. The husband was Sundarananda, half brother of the Buddha. When he looked down from the palace and saw the dignified form of the Buddha, he immediately came down and bowed to him. He took the Buddha's bowl into the palace and had it filled with food. However, when he presented it to the Buddha, the Buddha just kept on walking. Carrying the bowl, Sundarananda followed him to the place where he was staying. When they got there, the Buddha said to him, "The wealth you have in this world is like a floating cloud. If you continue to indulge yourself in sensual pleasures and engage in worldly affairs, you will end up being repeatedly reborn into the Six Destinies and never be released." Sundarananda was moved by these words, so even though his beautiful wife was waiting for him to return, he asked to become a monk and a follower of the Buddha.

After he became a monk, however, Sundarananda still missed his wife and family life. One day, he secretly contemplated going back to the palace. The Buddha knew what he was thinking. "I am taking the monks out to beg for alms. You can stay and look after the residence, but you have to clean the place up." Sundarananda readily agreed since he thought this would be a good chance to return to the palace. But the Buddha then asked him, "Are you planning to leave? Before you go, let me show you some things. You can leave afterwards if you still want to."

So the two of them sat down together. When the Buddha had entered into meditation, he led Sundarananda to heaven where there was a magnificent mansion. Upon seeing it, Sundarananda asked the Buddha with amazement, "How could there be such a beautiful building in the world?"

"Go over and ask who the owner is," the Buddha told him.

Sundarananda approached the mansion and saw that there were many beautiful women inside, so he asked them, "Who is your master?"

"Sundarananda, Sakyamuni Buddha's disciple," they replied. "When he departs from the human world, he will be reborn here and will become the master of this house."

Sundarananda was overjoyed to hear this. The Buddha asked him, "Well, what do you think? Aren't these women beautiful?"

"Oh, yes! They're gorgeous!"

"And how are they compared to your wife?"

"My wife is like a monkey in comparison to them! They are truly beautiful!"

"If you conduct your spiritual cultivation in earnest, you will be the master of this building some day." Sundarananda was exultant.

The Buddha then led him down to hell. Sundarananda saw all sorts of hell wardens, such as "cattle head" and "horse face," and he saw how the people in hell were horribly tortured. When Sundarananda saw a large boiler filled with oil, he was filled with terror. "This is horrible! This boiler hasn't been used yet. I wonder who it's for?" The Buddha told him to ask the warden in charge, who then replied, "This pot is being heated for the Buddha's disciple, Sundarananda. He still has sensual desires and might break the precepts. This boiler is where he will be when he falls into hell after his death. He will suffer from the burning flame and the boiling oil." This gave Sundarananda such a fright that he broke out in cold sweat.

"Now I know that heaven and hell exist, and they are created by my own mind," he told the Buddha. "From now on I will control my thoughts and study your teachings tirelessly."

It is all in the mind. Sometimes when we are in a situation, we cannot see clearly and are unable to control our desires or change our habits. Just like Sundarananda, it was not until he had been shown the whole picture and the consequences that he realized the

Buddhist concept, "The shore is where you turn around"—i.e., when you stop pursuing your desires, you will reach the end of suffering. Not everyone has the Buddha's ability to show Sundarananda both heaven and hell, and not everyone has Sundarananda's good fortune to meet someone as wise and powerful as the Buddha. This is why the Buddha said that it was difficult to enlighten people at the right occasion.

Even though Sundarananda was by the Buddha's side, he still had uncontrollable desires. It was not until he had witnessed both heaven and hell that he finally concentrated on his spiritual cultivation. If he had not seen these realms for himself, how would he have eliminated all sensual desires from his mind?

Learning Buddhism means that we must have control over our minds. Sometimes we have a diligent mindset, sometimes a slack one. When we are diligent, we will make progress; when we are slack, we will fall behind. Nevertheless, as long as we can learn the Buddha's teachings with sincerity, we will reform ourselves and also help others to attain enlightenment. Thus, we must earnestly and ceaselessly cherish the sincerity to study Buddhism.

IT IS DIFFICULT
NOT TO BE DISTURBED
BY EXTERNAL CONDITIONS

W hen the Buddha pointed out this nineteenth difficulty, he meant that it was truly difficult for people to be unaffected by the circumstances around them, whether adverse or favorable.

I remember we once held a gathering of Tzu Chi commissioners in Hualien. Thousands of people came from all parts of Taiwan to participate in the event. There were so many people that the original venue, the lobby of the Tzu Chi General Hospital, could not accommodate everyone. The gathering place was therefore moved to the basement of the Still Thoughts Hall. Since the building was still under construction, the audio and ventilation facilities were not functioning very well. To make matters worse, it was very hot that day, so the basement became an even less ideal place for a big gathering to be held.

Modern people are used to the niceties of life. To live in comfortable coolness in summer, they turn on the air conditioners in their homes and cars. Now, on a hot day, they had to stay in a crowded, badly ventilated environment. And although everyone came eager to gain a better understanding of Tzu Chi, they could not help being affected by the heat and stuffiness of the environment and so many of them lost their ability to concentrate. Thus, in a situation like this, the mind is influenced by external conditions.

IT IS DIFFICULT BECAUSE WE CANNOT ENDURE SUFFERING IN ORDER TO RECEIVE BUDDHIST TEACHINGS

Modern people can write beautifully, but with only superficial understanding of ideas, not going beyond the surface meaning expressed by words. People in the past were able to perceive deeper truths. They would "Travel thousands of miles in search of a teacher and journey tens of thousands of miles to learn a craft." Hui Ke, the second patriarch of the Zen sect in China, wanted to seek "our original self before we were born." In order to obtain the answer to his question from a great teacher, he willingly knelt in the snow for seven days and seven nights and amputated one arm to demonstrate his determination. In the end, he got the answer he wanted from his master: "Think not of what comes before and think not of what comes after—that is your original self before birth!" He grasped the truth contained

197

in the aphorism at that very instant and gained the unchanging will to pursue the Way. In stark contrast are the modern people whose minds cannot be steadied even after thousands of sutras and ideas have been imparted to them.

Hui Ke walked thousands of miles and knelt down for seven days to hear one wise sentence, but the truth contained in that one sentence was enough for a lifetime. His concentration was so great that the snow and the loss of an arm could not sway it. Under the most adverse circumstances, he still focused on the pursuit of the way to enlightenment. The reason that modern people fail to comprehend wonderful teachings is that they cannot give up their desires and pleasures, much less endure hardship. Therefore, their minds change with external conditions.

On the other hand, look at the Buddha, who was Prince Siddhartha before he achieved enlightenment. As crown prince, he enjoyed the veneration of all. His father, the king, had a "Three-Season Palace" built for him so he could always enjoy the pleasant weather of spring. Siddhartha had the love of his father and his people. But he did not let prestige and wealth confine his mind. Resolutely, he left everything behind and set out on his journey of spiritual cultivation.

During his five-year travels around the world and six years of ascetic living, he endured much suffering: coldness that no one else could bear and hunger that no one else could stand. For a total of eleven years, he weathered the adversities with great perseverance. During the final stage of his spiritual cultivation, he sat under a bodhi tree. Demons came to harass him, but he was able to subdue them all. Even the most attractive female demons could not tempt him. His mind remained unmoved by what he saw and his determination grew stronger as the temptations became greater. Finally, he passed all the tests and became a buddha. Afterwards, the Buddha followed his vow and painstakingly lectured to people on both sides of the Ganges River in order to enlighten them.

GREED CAN CAUSE DEATH

One day, the Buddha and Ananda were walking along a path when suddenly the Buddha said, "Ananda, there are some poisonous snakes!"

Ananda thought that there really were poisonous snakes and when he looked, he saw that the Buddha was referring to a pile of glistening silver coins. But Ananda replied, "Indeed, they are poisonous snakes." Then they walked on as though they had seen nothing.

Behind them were a father and son who heard what the Buddha and Ananda had said, so they also took a look, "Wow! There are no poisonous snakes, this is a pile of silver coins!"

Father and son were tempted, so the father told the son, "Quick! Let's take them home! We'll be rich!" So they hastily carried the coins home.

In fact, the silver coins had been stolen from the national treasury. The thieves had hidden the coins where the Buddha and Ananda found them and were planning to retrieve them after things cooled down. Little did they expect that someone would discover the coins and take them.

In the city, the government had already posted orders for the arrest of the criminals. Coins in the national treasury were always marked to indicate that they were national property. So when the father and son tried to use the coins in the market, they were taken for the thieves and arrested on the spot. Since stealing from the national treasury was a capital offense, the father and son were given the death sentence and taken to the execution ground. As they were about to be executed, the father sighed heavily and said to his son, "Son, they truly were poisonous snakes, and we were bitten by them!"

The executioner heard this and was puzzled by the man's words, so he reported the affair to the king. The king knew that there was profound meaning to those words and that they could not have come from a farmer's mouth, so he ordered the father and son to be brought before him. After personally questioning them, the king finally got an account of what had actually taken place. The king was a devout Buddhist and felt that when a person had the chance to hear the Buddha's speech, whether that person understood it or not, that person must have some kind of tie with the Buddha. Since these two only found the money by accident and did not actually steal it, the king pardoned them.

Whether we are affected by temptations depends on the greed in our hearts. To remain unmoved by something valuable is truly difficult for ordinary people. Like the father and son who saw the silver coins, how could they not be tempted? On the other hand, the Buddha and Ananda not only were not tempted, but saw the silver coins as poisonous snakes and stayed far away from them. This is the difference between sages and ordinary people. Also, ordinary people who are used to living comfortably find it hard to accept and endure life under bad conditions. A slight change in the weather disturbs their minds: when it is hot, they cannot sit still and are unable to concentrate. These are the reactions to the external world that belong to the level of the ordinary. It is no easy accomplishment to remain undisturbed by exterior conditions.

When people attend lectures on Buddhism, they think that they understand the concepts and feel sure that they will practice them. But after they leave the lecture hall, they fall back into their old bad habits again. Though they know that they should not harbor greed, anger or delusion, and that the fire of anger will destroy the merits that they have accumulated, when something doesn't go the way they want it to, they still flare up in rage. The mind of the common person is easily warped by outward influences. Even though they had determined to study Buddhism with diligence and seemed to be nearing the level of the Buddha, they will fall right back to the realm of the ordinary when their minds are moved by temptations or external events.

When we are learning to behave like the Buddha, we want to acquire control over our minds, so that we can be self-sufficient and free of any extraneous restrictions. However, the minds of ordinary people are often bound up by the environment that they are in. They are led into futile worldly pursuits that land them in the realm of the mundane. Thus, they can never be freed from the endless reincarnation into the Six Destinies of heaven, human, Asura, animal, hungry ghost and hell.

ENDLESS REINCARNATION RESULTS FROM GREED, ANGER AND DELUSION

We are reborn into different destinies based on the good or evil in us. If we have minds that want to do good, we will ascend to heaven. If we maintain decent minds and proper conduct, we will be reborn as humans. We will become pugnacious Asuras if we harbor anger and hatred in our minds. Evil mere thoughts of killing, stealing or fornicating will drag us down to hell. Greedy hearts will land us in the realm of hungry ghosts. Finally, if we are unchaste or incestuous, we will be reincarnated as animals. It is our minds that determine what realms we will reside in. Yet our minds are moved by the external world and we cannot fully concentrate on our spiritual cultivation, so we cannot reach enlightenment and transcend the Six Destinies.

Why is the mind influenced by external events? To explain it simply, it is because of the three poisons of greed, anger and delusion. If we are greedy, we will succumb easily to temptation. People greedy for carnal pleasure will be lured by attractive people of the opposite sex and forget themselves. As a result, families might be destroyed or bankrupted, and lust turned into hate might even lead to murderous intentions. Such are the consequences when the mind is moved by lustful desires.

As to greed for money, we must realize that money itself is harmless. It is the desire to illicitly procure it that is harmful. The glitter of silver coins is a natural attribute of the material, not a snare for people's minds. It is the mind that finds the glistening silver desirable and is captivated by it. Greed for money will lead to restless minds or, in the worst case, even insanity. In fact, many people who gamble or speculate in the stock market have suffered mental illness due to losses or falling prices. Some have even lost their families or committed suicide. Greed has become a very real cause of social problems.

Once when I was in Taichung, a reporter came to see me early in the morning. She told me that the stock market had enthralled many people. Once when she was conducting an interview at a hospital in Changhua, she happened to see more than ten mental patients being transferred from another hospital. That hospital already had too many patients and did not have any more rooms available. Also, the doctors were all very busy at the time and could not tend to the patients. One of the medical staff went to ask the director what to do with these new patients.

"That's easy," the director said. "Go get a board and write on it that stock values have gone sky-high, and then hang the board on the wall. That should solve the problem."

This prescription proved quite useful. All the patients where overjoyed when they saw the board on the wall. Everyone clapped their hands and laughed joyfully. Afterwards, some of the patients fell peacefully asleep, and some appeared to have become less disturbed. When stock prices rose, the patients were well; when prices went down, the patients fell ill. And all this over a number! For people with greed in their hearts, there are traps everywhere waiting to snare them.

Someone once said, "Beauty does not entrap people, people entrap themselves; wealth does not harm people, people harm themselves." Wise people are unconcerned with wealth, sensual enjoyment, prestige and self-interest. They are able to expand their personal emotions to a pure and lasting great love. We were fortunate enough to be born into this world as human beings and to be endowed with feelings and emotions. Let us not waste our emotions on worldly pursuits of material goods, but instead use the feelings of love and compassion to contribute to the well-being of all people. This is the wisdom of the bodhisattvas.

IT IS DIFFICULT
TO UNDERSTAND THE DIFFERENT WAYS
OF SPIRITUAL CULTIVATION

I f we are serious about learning Buddhism, we must seek to discover our genuine nature with an enlightened heart. Of course, this is not easy. But if we can bring Buddhist teachings into our daily lives and put the concepts into practice, then all our conduct becomes a wonderful method of cultivation through which we can gradually find our true nature. A prerequisite for beholding our nature and attaining enlightenment is to understand the true function of the methods of spiritual cultivation.

Buddhist monks and nuns begin their morning sessions every morning at four, during which they chant the sutras, prostrate themselves before statues of the Buddha and meditate. Should all students of Buddhism do the same? Must we also get up early in the morning and recite Buddhist sutras? Actually, rising early is a practical and appropriate approach to spiritual cultivation and also a good habit, for in this way we do not waste the best time of day. I often say that we must cherish every second of our lives, because the Buddha once said, "Life exists in the space of a breath." While we are able to breathe in and out, we are alive; without that one breath, life ends. Such is the fragile and impermanent nature of life that we really ought to cherish every single moment of it. If we have no clear direction and go through life like tourists casually sightseeing, then life will be wasted away in idle pursuits.

To Be Awake Is to Make Use of One's Abilities

The Buddha wanted his students to be awake every moment. To be "awake" means to be aware of our abilities and to use them to do what we can for other people. The Buddha wished for us to have more time to put our abilities to good use. One way to gain more time is to spend less time sleeping. This is why we should rise early in the morning, when we have the pure spirit and renewed energy to study and absorb Buddhist teachings.

If we sleep till seven or eight in the morning, then we have three or four hours less to use than if we got up at four. There are only twenty-four hours in a day. We use up eight to nine hours sleeping, and in the remaining hours we must eat and drink, and seek recreation and rest. Thus, how much time is left for us to really do something meaningful and to make good use of our life? Therefore, we should try our best to rise early, because by so doing we begin a day when it is still fresh and can study and absorb wisdom with maximum results. This is why every convent has its morning prayers at daybreak.

PROSTRATION BENEFITS THE BODY AND MIND

Is it necessary for Buddhists to prostrate themselves before statues?

Let us examine the practice closely. Prostration is beneficial for us in two ways: it exercises both our bodies and our minds. A person may be willing to rise early to study Buddhism, but unwilling to prostrate himself or herself before a statue of the Buddha. "I harbor reverence in my heart, so why must I prostrate myself to show that?" is the common response. For daily exercise, such people prefer a walk or some other form of activity to prostration. What is the difference between taking a walk and prostrating oneself before a statue? When we take a walk, our thoughts easily wander off; and since we usually walk with others, we start gossiping about other people. As we exercise our bodies, we create bad karma with the words we speak and our minds are disturbed from hearing so much criticism about others. Thus, while we exercise, our hearts and words become defiled.

When we prostrate ourselves before a statue of the Buddha, physically we are exercising, verbally we are reciting the Buddha's name, and mentally we are visualizing and reflecting upon the Buddha's teachings, reminding ourselves to follow the spirit and footsteps of the buddhas and bodhisattvas. The difference between people who prostrate themselves before the statues and the early risers who perform other physical exercises lies in their spiritual activity and the karma created by their words. Prostration is good for our physical health, and it increases our wisdom and strengthens our mental health. As we prostrate ourselves, we look at the statue, say the Buddha's name, and reflect on Buddhist teachings. Through this process, which is a method of spiritual cultivation, we gradually develop our wisdom. This is what we call a "convenient" or "expedient" method of learning Buddhism, a form of physical cultivation that is performed repeatedly to help us understand Buddhist concepts. We must understand the real function of these methods when we practice them in our daily lives, or we may cause our spiritual world to become closed and confused.

IT IS IMPORTANT TO UNDERSTAND THE CONVENIENT METHODS

I once knew a young wife who did not understand the true purpose of the methods of spiritual cultivation. She went to many temples and followed many Buddhist masters, but failed to take care of her own family. Every day, after her husband and children left for work and school, she would leave for the temples, neglecting her household duties. When her husband asked her why she had not made anything for the children to eat, she would go out and buy box lunches, just so that there would be something on the dinner table. When her husband told her that the children needed clean socks to wear every day and she should do the laundry, she simply went out and bought dozens of socks so the children would have a large supply of them.

But what kept her so busy that she didn't have time to spare for her family? She was busy attending

Buddhist lectures, reciting sutras, visiting different temples and tending to the masters. Indeed, she was very busy. And did all her efforts contribute to a more profound understanding of Buddhism? I don't think so. It is commonly said that "Being close to the Three Treasures—the Buddha, the dharma and the sangha—is meritorious, and prostrating oneself before statues of the Buddha and reciting the sutras inspires wisdom." This is what she firmly adhered to, but she failed to understand that these are only outward methods of spiritual cultivation and that to be truly enlightened she must reflect on her actions and study what the teachings truly mean.

Recitation of sutras and prostration before statues are religious practices and ceremonies. The purpose of reciting sutras is to understand the teachings of the Buddha, to know how to walk the path of life so we don't go astray. As for prostration, it is an expression of our respect for our spiritual teacher and his great wisdom. These methods of spiritual cultivation are both convenient and very important. Through repeated and continual practice, these methods enable us to understand Buddhist concepts and help inspire our pure true nature. If we fail to realize that they are only methods, not goals in themselves, and do nothing else to cultivate our minds, then we will end up like that young wife whose efforts were superficial and would only result in a superficial understanding of Buddhism.

Human beings all cling to something. Some people hang on to practicalities and some hold fast to theories, neither able to blend theory with practice. Thus, people either practice something without knowing why, or know all the theories but fail to put them into practice. These are the difficulties concerning the understanding of those convenient methods. If people are able to reach a subtle balance between practicing and reasoning, then nothing will be too difficult to accomplish and no hindrance will be so great that it can't be overcome.

In a passage in the *Diamond Sutra*, the Buddha says: "Know that my teachings are like a raft that will ferry you across the river of suffering. After you have reached the shore of nirvana, you should let go of these teachings. If the teachings that lead you to nirvana can be cast away, then other teachings which were never of practical use to you certainly should also be cast away."

We can't carry the raft on our backs after we have sailed across the river, can we? All the teachings we hear and all the religious practices are convenient methods. Through the unreal, impermanent forms of our physical actions, we gain the true supreme wisdom and understand the truth. Once we understand the true meaning of the convenient methods, then there is no difficulty we cannot overcome. We will comprehend all teachings and our wisdom will be as vast as the ocean.

EPILOGUE
THE PATH OF THE BODHISATTVAS

P eople have different expectations of themselves, and in society the dissimilarity between individuals is easily visible. I hope that Tzu Chi will be an organization that transcends this world, and that its members will share a common spirit and outlook. What is this common spirit that we should have? We look to the buddhas and bodhisattvas and seek to develop a pure quality and spirit that is akin to theirs.

The *Three-Character Classic* [the first primer for Chinese students before formal schooling] opens with the following words, "At birth, human nature is good; our nature is similar, our acquired behavior disparate." The reason that people depart from their original good nature is because they develop different habits. What we want to do is to return to our original nature, which requires much practice. The only way to transcend the temperament of the common person is to emulate the virtue and conduct of the Buddha and bodhisattvas.

THE SPIRIT OF THE TZU CHI BODHISATTVAS

When the Buddha was first cultivating himself, he once saved a little bird by feeding his own flesh to the hawk that had caught it. To free the little bird without starving the hawk, he cut off enough flesh that would weigh the same as the little bird. Even if he had had to give up all his flesh, his intention would have remained firm.

Our shared ideal should be to learn from the genuinely good deeds that the Buddha did when he was still a bodhisattva who was willing to slice off his own flesh to save another living being. For the sake of all living beings and for our mission of charity, which is to be carried out over the centuries, we should emulate the spirit of the bodhisattvas. Do not think despairingly, "I am tired of practicing good deeds. I am tired of trying to make myself heard." In fact, to become a bodhisattva, we must not only talk and yell tirelessly, but also walk and act indefatigably. Even if it means shedding blood by cutting our own flesh, we still have to go on.

In learning Buddhism, our thoughts, words and deeds must be in conformity. Since we have resolved to pursue Buddhism, we should persevere to the very end. We must not be frustrated by any difficulty and say, "Aw, I don't want to be a Buddhist any more!"

For words of despair are easy to utter, but once you say them, your determination to pursue Buddhism will quickly dwindle. Why is this? Because the body, mind and mouth are one. The words uttered through the mouth are the mind's thoughts, and when the mind falters, obstacles will appear immediately. Therefore it is essential that we control our minds and thoughts.

High mountains are hard to conquer. Halfway up, the mountain cliff may become steeper and more rugged. If we despair of the long journey ahead and lose our grip, we might plummet into the valley. Although the ascent to the top is extremely demanding, with every effort you make, you will advance a little. With perseverance, you will finally reach the summit. If you think even once of giving up or becoming angry, your grip will loosen and you will fall.

As students of Buddhism, we must pay close attention to body, mouth and mind. In daily life, no matter what kind of hardship confronts us, we must remain optimistic and say, "I want to continue," and, like the mountain-climber, never rest until we reach the top.

MUTUAL ENCOURAGEMENT AND STIMULATION

It is common for people to encourage and stimulate each other. To encourage means to offer good advice patiently, like books that contain inspiring articles. Stimulation means to spur one's mind with adversity, to test whether our will to pursue Buddhism is unchangeable and our words uncomplaining. Only if we are truly determined and uncomplaining will we be able to learn the pure, good actions of the bodhisattva.

When we learn Buddhism, we must rid ourselves of our bad habits, return to our original nature, and achieve the level of the Buddha. We must face adversity with courage and not let our minds fall into the level of the mundane, or worse the realm of the Asuras. Into which of the Six Destinies we are reborn depends on our thoughts, and with a single thought we can either advance or regress. If we keep oscillating back and forth, then we will forever be turning in the great cycle and never be freed from eternal reincarnation.

We are rarely born as human beings, the Buddhist teachings are valuable knowledge, and the Path of the Bodhisattvas is hard to find. We were fortunate enough in this life to be endowed with human forms, to have learned the Buddhist teachings, and to be traveling on the Path of the Bodhisattvas. Let us not take one step forward and fall one step behind, but rather let us advance steadily forward. Do not relax, because once you slacken it will be very difficult to start over again. On the Path of the Bodhisattvas, we must be cautious as to what we think, say and do, and encourage and stimulate each other.

Adversity is a book that teaches without words, presented before us as it is. Let us use it to test how well we have cultivated ourselves and remind ourselves to be sincere in our studies. Let us change the environment with our minds, and not let our hearts be altered by the things around us.